Nested Transactions

MIT Press Series in Information Systems
Michael Lesk, editor

Nested Transactions: An Approach to Reliable Distributed Computing, by J. Eliot B. Moss, 1985

Nested Transactions
An Approach to Reliable Distributed Computing

J. Eliot B. Moss

The MIT Press
Cambridge, Massachusetts
London, England

This book was printed and bound in the United States of America.

Publisher's Note: This format is intended to reduce the cost of publishing certain works in book form and to shorten the gap between editorial preparation and final publication. Detailed editing and composition have been avoided by photographing the text of this book directly from the author's camera-ready copy.

Library of Congress Cataloging in Publication Data

Moss, J. Eliot B.
Nested transactions.

(The MIT Press series in information systems)
Bibliography: p.
Includes index.
1. Electronic data processing—Distributed processing
—Reliability. I. Title. II. Series.
QA76.9.D5M67 1985 001.64 84-19428
ISBN 0-262-13200-1

To Hannah: May she also be published before long.

Contents

Series Foreword

This book begins the MIT Press series in Information Systems. As we enter the "information age," understanding the technology of information handling becomes essential to scientists and engineers. Systems that store, manipulate, and retrieve all kinds of information, including numbers, text, and pictures, are now common. Their design, their interconnections, and their use are all important research topics.

For some time, computers have dominated numerical processing; recently they have taken over text preparation, and they are moving in on graphics. As more and more kinds of data are computer processed, hardware, algorithms, languages, and techniques for data handling become even more important. As information systems spread into new domains, new problems arise in their construction. Specific applications are often built with specific techniques based on detailed knowledge of that particular application area. We must both extract the general principles and learn how to efficiently implement the specific details in order to make information systems better and faster in the future.

The purpose of this series, then, is to record information about information systems. The MIT Press will publish both new research contributions and summaries of the state of the art, wherever such books are well written, informative, and useful to their audience. Technical excellence will be the primary criterion.

It is appropriate to begin this series with *Nested Transactions* by J. Eliot B. Moss, since this book deals with the fundamental architecture of information systems. As computers become cheaper, centralizing them becomes pointless, and both logically and geographically distributed computing is spreading quickly. Synchronizing events in these separated computers, however, is both essential and difficult, even when every part is working. When some parts of the system are broken, distributed computing becomes even more complicated.

The reader will find here a design for programming a reliable distributed system, based on nested transactions. The techniques explained are applicable in areas ranging from data bases to network design. This book is remarkable for its clarity, its reasonable recommendations, and its importance to the future of systems architecture.

Michael Lesk

Acknowledgments

First, the ideas leading to the thesis on which this work is based were aided greatly by discussions with a number of people at the Laboratory for Computer Science, especially in the Distributed Systems Group (now the Argus project). Sometimes it is hard to say where my ideas stop and theirs begin.

Next, several people were helpful in the actual production of the book: Tyrone Sealy, for messing with a lot of backup tapes, not to mention his traditional Dover tuning; Bob Scheifler for on-site printing; Anne Rubin for mailing; Michael Thompson for private courier service; and especially Hannah Abbott for redoing the figures to improve the quality. The Army War College has been helpful by lending moral support, and through the services of the Reprographics Division. The MIT Laboratory for Computer Science made this edition possible by permitting use of the services of their personnel and equipment. I am very grateful for their continuing support.

Perhaps more important than production is the advocacy of my thesis adviser, Barbara Liskov. It was because of her that The MIT Press considered the project. I also appreciate the reviewers' comments, which enabled me to substantially improve the work without undertaking a complete rewrite.

Last, I would like to thank my colleagues at the War College, my friends, and my wife, for being understanding during the time it took to prepare the manuscript for publication.

Nested Transactions

1. Introduction.

It seems that every day there are more news reports and product announcements for personal computers, home computers, and computer communications equipment. Indications are that distributed computing will become more and more common, perhaps with the end result that almost everyone will have a computer that is connected in one way or another with many other computers. Just as most people have a telephone and depend on it, the same may happen with computers. Undoubtedly such universal use of computers and rapid exchange of information will have a dramatic impact: social, economic, and political. Distributed computing will then be a fact of life and important to everyone.

This report is concerned not with the effects of the distributed computing revolution, but with a crucial technical problem: how to build a reliable distributed computing system. When one assembles a large number of devices (such as computers) into a system, one gets both higher and lower reliability simultaneously: lower reliability in the sense that it is more likely that at least one component fails at any given time; higher reliability in the sense that it is more likely that at least one component is working at any given time. The point is that for a large system to operate effectively, it is important that most components continue to work even while others are broken. That is, the system must not count on having all its components working at once. It is generally understood how to build the hardware components so that hardware failures are mostly independent.

Because hardware and its failure properties are already fairly well understood, we will not examine hardware issues very deeply. Rather, we will be concerned mainly with the software aspects of achieving reliable operation of a system of computers that communicate via a network. The goal of our research was to design a system for reliable distributed computing. In particular, the system should survive processor failures (crashes) and communications problems (e.g., lost, duplicated, and delayed messages). While the reader must be the final judge, we believe that we have met our goal. Further, our design is novel in that it supports nested transactions in a new way. What nested transactions are, and the ways in which our approach is new we explain below.

1.1 The Approach.

The approach we have taken to the problem of writing software for an unreliable system is based on the idea of *transactions*. The word *transaction* has been used in many different ways in different contexts. The meaning we intend for *transaction* is *atomic action*: an atomic action is some computation that changes or reads the state of one or more data objects and *appears* to take place indivisibly. That is, an atomic action always performs as if it is run in isolation and to completion.

A major problem solved by using transactions is preserving the integrity of data stored within a computer system. Of course the software technique of transactions must be complemented by sufficient hardware redundancy - otherwise hardware failures might destroy all copies of important data. The two main ways in which transactions help preserve data integrity are *failure atomicity* and *synchronization*. Synchronization is represented by the fact that two different transactions always appear to have happened sequentially. Sequentiality is important when the transactions access or modify some of the same data objects. In short, synchronization insures that inconsistencies do not arise because of concurrent access to data.

Failure atomicity is the property that a transaction either happens in entirety or not at all, even if there are partial system failures while processing the transaction. A common example demonstrating the importance of failure atomicity is electronic funds transfer. A transfer involves two operations: decrementing one account and incrementing another. If just one of the two operations is performed, somebody has lost money (either a customer or the bank). However, money is correctly conserved if both operations happen, or neither. Atomic actions possess failure atomicity by definition.

Clearly it would be nice if atomic actions were directly available (built-in to the hardware). Unfortunately, very few hardware operations are atomic. It takes some clever design to build a system supporting atomic actions that can affect arbitrary subsets of the data stored in the system. Several such designs suitable for distributed systems have been implemented and many other approaches have been suggested. Our design builds on this earlier work.

The main result of this report is a novel implementation of *nested transactions*. Nested transactions are an extension of the more traditional notion of transactions. The difference between transactions and nested transactions is that nested transactions have more internal structure. A transaction is just a group of *primitive actions* (e.g., reads and writes of simple data objects) that are performed as a unit. Nested transactions have a hierarchical grouping structure: each nested transaction consists of either primitive actions or some nested transactions (called *subtransactions* of the containing nested transaction).

Nested transactions have at least two advantages over simple (single-level) transactions. First, subtransactions of a nested transaction fail independently of each other and independently of the containing transaction. This allows possibilities such as attempting a piece of a computation at one computer and redoing only that piece if the computer fails. In the single-level transaction system, if any piece fails, the whole transaction fails. The second advantage of nested transactions is that they provide appropriate synchronization between concurrently running parts of the same nested transaction. This implies that more work can be processed concurrently with confidence that inconsistencies will not arise through improper concurrent access to data. Because nested transactions provide correct synchronization within a transaction, it is easy to compose a number of previously existing transactions into a new transaction without danger of inconsistency arising from concurrent access to the same data object by two or more of the composed transactions.

1.2 Points of Novelty.

Our nested transaction system uses locking for synchronization, and is the first design to do so. Reed [Reed78] presented the first comprehensive design of a nested transaction system, but his design uses timestamps for synchronization. Our system and his deal with deadlock in different ways, too. The idea of nested transactions seems to have originated with Davies [Davies73] some time ago, but no designs incorporated the idea until recently.

The novel material of this report is presented in three pieces. The first part develops the locking algorithm for nested transactions and also an algorithm for restoring data when a transaction fails and has to be undone. The second part is concerned with the algorithm for managing nested transactions in a distributed system. The third part deals with the issue of progress in the system, and presents a new deadlock detection algorithm. In sum, the new work presented in this report culminates in four algorithms that handle nested transactions:

- A locking algorithm.
- An object state restoration algorithm.
- A distributed transaction management algorithm.
- A distributed deadlock detection algorithm.

1.3 Overview of Related Work.

As with any piece of research, our work has built on the work of many others. We make a number of specific citations throughout the report, and devote Chapter 7 entirely to discussion of related work. Here is a short summary of some of the more closely related research. Our locking method is an extension of the well-known two-phase locking protocol [EGLT76] used in many systems (e.g., [Gray78, IMS78, LeLann81]). Our object state restoration (transaction undo) algorithm is also based on methods used in many systems (e.g., [Gray78, IMS78, SMB79, Paxton79, LeLann81]). The distributed transaction management algorithm is original, except in its incorporation of a two-phase commit protocol [Gray78, Gray80a, Paxton79, IMS78, Reed78, LeLann81, Lindsay79, HS80]. The distributed deadlock detection algorithm is an extension of work reported in [Goldman77] and [Obermarck80]. Some of the methods of presentation that we have used derive from other specific works. In particular, the system model and failure model of Chapter 2 was inspired by [LS], and the discussion of transaction semantics in Chapter 3 is based on [EGLT76] and [Gray78].

1.4 Plan of the Book.

Here is a brief review of the organization of this report. Chapter 2 presents a model for distributed systems, including their failure properties; it is the only chapter containing significant discussion of hardware. Chapter 3 discusses the idea of transactions in some detail, including some simple algorithms for locking, state restoration, and two-phase commit. The main purpose of Chapters 2 and 3 are to set the stage for the technical exposition of Chapters 4, 5, and 6.

Chapter 4 introduces the idea of nested transactions and explores it in some detail. Chapter 4 is somewhat parallel to Chapter 3 in that it extends the locking and state restoration algorithms of Chapter 3 to nested transactions. Chapter 5 continues the implementation of nested transactions by showing how to run nested transactions in a distributed system, including the handling of failures. Chapter 6 builds on the techniques of Chapter 5, by showing how to detect deadlocks among nested transactions in a distributed system, and how to make a strong guarantee that any well-formed transaction request will be completed eventually.

Chapter 7 attempts to put our work in context through a discussion of related work. Chapter 8 presents a summary with some conclusions, and offers many suggestions for further research.

1.5 Relationship to the Thesis

This book is based on a thesis submitted in 1981 [Moss81], which was also released as a technical report. Much of the text is the same as in those documents. However, in addition to a number of minor corrections and adjustments, we have incorporated new material, taking into account the many and rapid developments of the three years since original publication. Chapter 4 has been changed somewhat, to make it simpler, as result of experience presenting the material to a number of audiences. Chapters 7 and 8 have been expanded to describe some significant new work. Further, we have included material concerning the concept of hierarchy, in an attempt to place nested transactions in a broader context. Finally, the bibliography has been expanded considerably. The thrust of the changes has been to make the book more useful to researchers and students desiring to learn about this quickly growing and exciting field of computer systems: transactions and distributed processing.

2. Modelling the Underlying System.

This chapter presents the foundation upon which a reliable distributed transaction system is built in later chapters. We will explain what we mean by a distributed system and go into some detail about our assumptions concerning processors, memories, and communication, including their failure properties. We will describe a model that encompasses the class of systems of interest and will give some justifications for the model. We will not be interested in *formal* properties of the model: the model's main purpose is to make our assumptions as clear as possible. Much of this chapter was inspired by Lampson and Sturgis [LS].

2.1 Modelling Failure.

When setting out to model failure, the first obstacle encountered is that there is no limit to severity of failure in reality. For example, while it might be very unlikely, it is possible that all components in the system might fail at once and break the system beyond repair. Any system cannot survive all possible failures - it will tolerate only certain sets of failures. Our approach is to make it plain which failures will be tolerated and which will not. Additionally, it is our goal that the intolerable failures can be made as rare as necessary, thus permitting an arbitrarily high (though not perfect) level of reliability to be achieved.

We divide the possible behaviors of a real system or component into two classes: acceptable and unacceptable. We *assume* that the unacceptable behaviors do not occur. The assumption that unacceptable behavior never happens is the basic assumption of the model of failure. As just explained, we are careful to insure that the unacceptable behaviors of the system can be made arbitrarily unlikely. Unacceptable behavior is intolerable, and system behavior is not constrained should an unacceptable situation arise. Acceptable behavior comes in two varieties: good (normal) behavior, and bad (undesirable, failing) but tolerable behavior. For short we call the three possible kinds of behavior good, tolerable, and intolerable.

Here is an example of these different kinds of behavior. Consider a memory with extra error detecting and correcting bits. Good behavior of the memory itself is to return the data previously stored. Tolerable behavior of a memory read is to return bad data such that the error correcting bits are sufficient to correct the error. Note that tolerable behavior at one level turns into good behavior at a higher level. In fact, behavior is tolerable *only* if it is turned into good behavior at a higher level. Intolerable behavior of a memory read is to return bad data such that the error correcting bits are either insufficient to correct the error, or the error is incorrectly "corrected", or there does not appear to be an error. Again, these behaviors are intolerable only because the system in which the memory is embedded cannot handle them. For example, some of the behaviors just classed as intolerable would be tolerable in a system employing duplicate or triplicate memory subsystems. Good behavior should be the most likely; intolerable behavior had better be the least likely.

2.2 Overview of the Model.

Our model of a distributed system is a number of *nodes* (abstract computers) that communicate only by sending *messages* over an (abstract) communications network, as shown in the diagram below. Each node consists of a processor and some memory; input/output is not modelled in detail. Nodes may go down (crash) and up (recover), and new nodes may be added to the network over time. No specific provisions are made for removing nodes from the network. However, removal is often equivalent to crashing, from the viewpoint of nodes still in the network. It is assumed that every pair of nodes can communicate in both directions, though perhaps not directly. We will describe nodes and their behavior, and then go on to the properties we assume about communication.

Distributed System Model

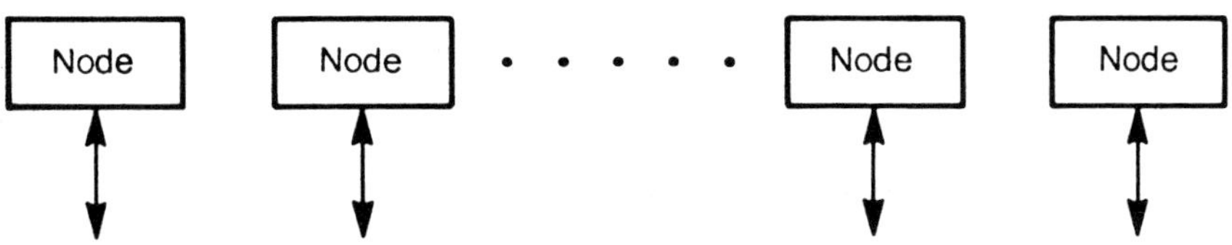

Communications Network
(no specific topology implied)

2.3 Nodes.

A node consists of a processor and some memory. An unusual feature of the node model is that there are two kinds of memory, called *permanent* and *volatile* (see the diagram below). It is assumed that the contents of volatile memory are lost in a crash and that the contents of permanent memory survives crashes. We will discuss the failure properties of nodes, go into some detail concerning permanent memory, and then consider the processor and volatile memory.

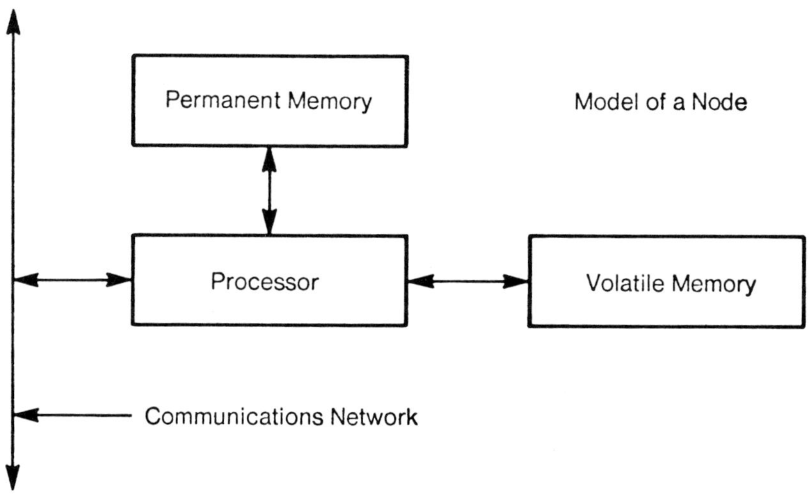

2.3.1 Node Failure.

The discussion of nodes is concerned mainly with failure properties. We model any processor or volatile memory failure as a node failure. A node failure is equivalent to stopping the processor, resetting the processor and volatile memory to a standard state, and starting the processor some time later. When a node fails, it is said to have *crashed*, and when it restarts, it is said to have *recovered*. Permanent memory never fails, and its state is not affected by crashes.

In sum, good behavior of a node is normal execution of steps by the processor and normal updating and retention of data by the memories. It is tolerable for a node to crash: the processor stops for some period of time, the volatile memory state is lost, and the permanent memory state is preserved. Any other behavior (e.g., a crashed processor writing into permanent memory or a crashed processor sending messages) is intolerable. Note that we do not permit nodes to stay down or be disconnected from the network forever. The algorithms of later chapters will not deal with permanent node failures.

Note that the term *volatile* indicates vulnerability to crashes, and does not mean that the contents of volatile memory does or does not survive loss of electrical power. Similarly *permanent* indicates the ability to survive node failures. However, as we will explain a little later, volatile memory will typically correspond (more or less) to the main memory of the system and permanent memory to the (usually somewhat separate) mass storage. The distinction between volatile and permanent memory may or may not be obvious to the programmer. However, the algorithms of later chapters require the ability of the transaction system to control when permanent memory is updated.

Programming errors are not addressed by the model. While some bugs may be detected in the normal course of affairs, it is assumed that the system is programmed correctly and is presented only with well-formed tasks to execute. Thus we relegate undetected programmer and operator errors to the intolerable category. We stress that the sort of reliability we strive for is correct execution of programs; insuring the correctness of the programs is beyond the scope of this work.

2.3.2 About Permanent Memory.

In our model the state of the system must be encoded in permanent memory, because permanent memory is the only part of the system state that survives node failures and thus permits the system to make progress. Because permanent memory is so important, we will examine its properties and some aspects of its implementation in more detail. Note that permanent storage has strict reliability constraints: its only tolerable behavior is to store and return information correctly, as commanded by the processor.

The crucial property of permanent memory is its reliability. There are two ways in which that reliability is achieved. First there is the inherent reliability (or lack of it) of the devices used to construct permanent memory. Second there is the way in which permanent memory is accessed. This latter property is a bit subtle and deserves further explanation. Permanent memory is updated carefully *because* of its importance. Furthermore, permanent memory is more likely to be implemented using mass storage (the large, slow, cheap end of the memory hierarchy), so it will be accessed as infrequently as possible. (Hence, in later chapters we will operate on the assumption that access to permanent memory is expensive.) Note that the infrequency of access to permanent memory actually enhances its reliability: it is less likely that a processor that has gone berserk will damage the contents of permanent memory. Nevertheless, though permanent memory would tend to correspond to mass memory and volatile memory to the main store, *permanent* and *volatile* reflect how the memory is used rather than its technology and speed of access. In particular, the parts of secondary memory that are used as a paging store or for scratch files will usually be volatile.

The stability (survival of failures) of permanent memory is necessary but not sufficient. We must also be able to update permanent memory atomically. For example, it is possible to perform reliable updates by writing new information in currently unused blocks, and once everything has been successfully written, change one block (or word, or even bit) to indicate that the update is complete. However the last update must be atomic - it must appear to happen completely or not at all, even if there is a failure while the update is occurring. Lampson and Sturgis [LS] have described a method for implementing atomic stable storage using magnetic disks. The key idea is to use two disk blocks to represent each block of data that must be updated atomically, and to update one and then the other. A number of systems use a less symmetric (though probably faster) technique: record the update on one or more magnetic tape logs before updating disk. See [Gray78] for further discussion of such methods.

Once we have the ability to update one block atomically, we can update atomically as many blocks as we want by clever organization of the data. For example, suppose all the interesting data in permanent memory is organized into a tree structure with a known distinguished block being the root of the tree. We can update as much data as we like atomically by writing updated data into free blocks, and inserting the new structure in the tree by atomically over-writing the special root block as the last step. Other techniques for large atomic updates have been devised; the point is that such updates are sometimes necessary and that they are possible.

While particular devices such as disks and tapes have been mentioned, permanent memory might be built with just about any memory devices. In fact, permanent memories have been constructed using semiconductor memory technology [BBP83]. Such designs are very useful when a fast buffer to a larger mass permanent memory is necessary to achieve sufficient performance. However, the key properties of permanent memory are stability (survival of failures) and atomic update. All schemes we have encountered include redundancy, because single failures are too common, and also because multiple physical updates are needed to achieve atomicity. All schemes also require special action after crashes, to flush partial updates, etc. In general, periodic scanning or copying of the data is necessary to avoid loss because of media degradation over time (such as demagnetization, chemical decomposition, etc.), though the use of media with higher reliability or more redundancy may obviate this requirement. Lastly, by increasing the number of copies of data that are stored, a good permanent memory design can achieve arbitrarily high reliability.

2.3.3 Processors.

The exact class of machines we would like to model is difficult to characterize, because we do not wish to rule out different arrangements with equivalent computing power. Therefore, we will not describe what a processor *is*, but what it can *do*. The essential property of a processor is that it can change the state of the volatile and permanent memories, and it can send and receive information on the communications network. We make no assumptions concerning the degree of concurrent activity in a processor. However, if there is concurrency, we must be able to build mutual exclusion locks or a similar synchronization primitive, to meet the synchronization requirements of later chapters.

Also, there must be a single value that bounds the rate at which any processor can change the state of its memories, or send or receive messages. This is an intuitively reasonable restriction that avoids obscure situations such as one processor performing an unbounded number of steps between two steps of another continuously running[1] processor. We will not be more explicit about what a "step" is, because an explanation is not necessary and might reduce the generality of the model.

An abstract node conforming to our model could be implemented with a single real processor or several real processors, or one real processor could implement several abstract nodes (via multiprogramming or even multiprocessing). It is even conceivable that an abstract node could "move" from one real processor to another, or that a diffuse collection of processors could cooperatively implement one or more nodes.

Permanent memory is the foundation of the system, and is the only part that we assume to be perfect. In contrast processors and volatile memory need not be anywhere near perfect. It is sufficient that there be no *undetected* errors in their actions. This is because a detected but uncorrectable error can simply be treated as a crash. It is crucial that a processor error not propagate to permanent memory or to other nodes via message passing. This last requirement is probably the weakest point of the failure model of the system, because typical processors are not reliable enough (most have no internal checking at all, except perhaps parity bits on microcode memory). However, though processors are often the weakest link, this need not be the case: it is possible to build processors that satisfy our assumptions, though more is involved than adding error correcting bits to memories. Further, one could just use the classical method: two or three processors performing the same computation with their results cross-checked continuously. We maintain that it is possible to reduce the probability of intolerable behavior in processors and volatile memories to arbitrarily low values.

---

1. Crashes can be indefinitely long. Hence an unbounded number of steps could be performed by one processor while another processor is crashed.

2.3.4 Discussion.

We have chosen a model consisting of extremely reliable permanent memory and unreliable processors and volatile memory. Why is this model appropriate? First, for purposes of argument it is convenient to have a reliable component (permanent memory in this case); otherwise it is hard to say anything interesting about the behavior of the system. A second reason that our node model is appropriate is that it is realistic - many current hardware configurations correspond to our idea of a node. Lastly, our model is appropriate because it is simple and very general. It should continue to apply for a long time, so our work will not soon be outdated by changes in hardware technology.

However, there are two objections to the model we would like to answer. First, why is there the dichotomy of permanent and volatile memory? One answer is that the dichotomy corresponds to the way systems are built. A better answer is that perfect and imperfect memories are the only kinds one can have, and that the perfect/imperfect distinction is the only useful distinction that can be made by software. Further, volatile and permanent memory form the simplest model that admits failure in a describable and realistic fashion.

The second objection is that every node must possess permanent memory. Actually, it is not necessary that each node have its own permanent memory. Some system functions might not require permanent storage and could be performed by processors without permanent memory. Also, it is reasonable for a processor lacking permanent memory to use the permanent memory of another processor by communicating with that processor through the network.

2.4 Modelling Communication.

The unit of communication in our model is the *message*. A message conveys a bit string from one node to another; we place no particular bound on the size of messages. A message is sent by one node to another specific node; we assume that any node can transmit a message to any other node. It may be possible to broadcast a message to a number of other nodes, but we view this as just an optimization of sending separate messages. The places where message broadcasting can be used to advantage in later algorithms will be obvious, so we will not discuss broadcast further. It is the job of the sender to insure that the message is meaningful to the recipient. Before discussing communications failure modes, we will first argue for the appropriateness of our model.

One objection that could be raised against our model is the bias toward messages (packet switching) instead of communications circuits or streams of bits (circuit switching). The answer is that both models of communication are equally powerful, that packet switching is sufficient, and that packet switching is more natural for the algorithms we will present in later chapters. Another objection is that we assume all nodes can communicate with all others. Actually, all we require is that any pair of nodes wishing to interact be able to send messages to each other (in both directions). However, it is *not* assumed that every node can communicate *directly* with every other node; message forwarding is permissible, and possibly necessary or desirable in many systems, for a variety of reasons. A final objection is that we permit messages of arbitrary length. To this objection we say that it is all right for the underlying system to split a message up into smaller pieces for transmission, and to reassemble the message before presenting it to the recipient. Further, it is difficult to bound the size of some of the messages sent in the protocols developed later. If necessary, explicit packetization could be added; we omitted packetization to make the algorithms simpler.

2.4.1 Modelling Communications Failures.

Here is a list of the bad things we permit to happen to a message:

- It may be lost entirely.
- It may be garbled, or only parts of it arrive.
- It may arrive out of order with respect to other messages from the same sender to the same recipient.
- It may be duplicated, and arrive more than once.
- It may be arbitrarily delayed.

It is intolerable for a message to be transformed from one good message into another good message. A good message is one with a good checksum.[1] Thus it is very unlikely for a good message to be turned into another good one, though it is *possible* for it to happen. But by using more and more checksum bits, the probability of the intolerable transformation can be made arbitrarily small. The destination address should be part of the checksummed data, so that delivery to the correct recipient can be guaranteed. Messages with bad checksums are simply discarded, so bad messages are eliminated from the model. We also assume that the communications network does not spontaneously generate (good) messages.

In sum, when a message message is sent, zero, one, or more copies of it will arrive at the destination, after arbitrary delays. However, no copies arrive elsewhere, and if a copy arrives, it arrives intact. Even finite recipient buffer space can be modelled: if a message arrives for which there is no room, it (or some other message in a queue) can be discarded. This solution can turn a good message into a lost message, but both are acceptable behaviors. We do assume that if a message is sent repeatedly, at least one good copy will eventually make it to the recipient. This assumption implies that the network never goes down forever. It also requires that the sender not send messages too large for the recipient ever to accept. However, some convention is required for any communication to take place. If necessary, the sender and recipient can use a protocol for allocation of buffer space.

Some people might object to the simplicity of the protocol: that we permit duplicates, out-of-order messages, etc., and that we include no automatic acknowledgments or flow control mechanisms. There are several defenses of this position. First, if we need protocols that make stronger guarantees, we will have to build them explicitly, which gives our work more credibility. Second, we will not need stronger properties very much in later chapters. But the best argument is that much of the same mechanism must necessarily be constructed in the high level protocols. This has been called the end-to-end argument [SRC81].

A typical example is elimination of duplicates. The system could automatically insure removal of duplicates, at some cost. However, higher-level protocols might very well initiate the same request more than once in response to a time-out. In terms of the semantics of the

---

1. If "goodness" of messages can be insured using some method other than checksums, then that would be all right.

application, the new messages are duplicates, because the desired actions should be performed only once. However, the messages may be distinct in terms of what the communications subsystem sees, so automatic duplicate removal will not eliminate the need for duplicate removal at the application level. Similar arguments apply to acknowledgments. The fact that messages may arrive out of order may not necessarily be defended by the end-to-end argument, but it turns out that it can be expensive to preserve message order, and we will not generally need it.

2.5 The System as a Whole.

While we have not done so, the system model we have presented could be formalized without much effort. However, the model would be incomplete if it did not insure that only causal (i.e., realizable) systems were modelled. To insure causality, we need to represent time and ordering relationships correctly. It is easy to define a reasonable notion of time at each local processor: time advances as the processor executes instructions. The correct notion of time for a distributed system is complicated by relativistic effects. It is convenient to introduce the notion of an omniscient observer. Each such observer perceives all events of the system, though different observers may see the same events happen in different orders. We can characterize the behavior of the system by describing the constraints that apply to all observers. The constraints are simple:

- The order of all events occurring at a single node will be perceived in the same order everywhere, though events occurring at different nodes may be seen to occur in different orders.
- The sending of a particular message will always be perceived as occurring before it is received. Further, all observers will agree on the number of copies of the message delivered.

The above constraints are necessary, for otherwise the system might be non-causal or otherwise inconsistent with physical law. More constraints would apply to any given system or configuration, such as minimum communication delays based on the travel time of light between nodes. However, the above constraints seem to be sufficient for arguing the partial correctness of distributed programs that do not refer to real time, because all necessary causal relations are stated.

2.6 Summary.

Our model of a distributed system is a collection of nodes, where each node consists of a processor with volatile and permanent memory. It is permissible for one node's permanent memory to be implemented elsewhere and used via message passing. One could also use nodes lacking permanent memory for computation only. Processor crashes merely wipe out the volatile memory, leaving the permanent memory intact. A node may not crash forever. New nodes may enter the system. There is no *a priori* bound on the number of nodes in the system.

Messages are the means of communication. A message is sent from a node to a particular recipient node, and may arrive zero, one, or more times, with arbitrary delay. Its order of receipt with respect to other messages is unspecified, and the different copies may mix in arbitrarily. However, messages arrive intact if at all, and are never delivered to the wrong recipient.

Perhaps most important is the general approach to dealing with failures in an organized fashion. We split device behaviors into three categories: good behavior, faulty but tolerable behavior, and intolerable (unhandled) failure. Further, we seek a design in which the probability of intolerable behavior can be made arbitrarily small. This permits one to build a system that is as reliable as desired, from a hardware standpoint, if one is willing to dedicate the necessary resources. We do not tackle the thorny problem of software errors.

3. Transactions.

The goal of our work is to design a system for reliably manipulating stored data in distributed systems. The previous chapter defined "distributed system". Now we will discuss what we mean by "reliably manipulating stored data". This chapter does not introduce novel material - it continues to build the conceptual foundation necessary for understanding the following three chapters.

3.1 Fundamental Concepts.

We will now describe the basic ideas that give rise to the use of transactions as concepts and tools.

3.1.1 Consistency.

If the data stored in the system has any *a priori* constraints, we wish to guarantee that they will never be violated (assuming all the programs to be correct, of course). A typical example of such a constraint is that the sum of the balances of all the accounts in a bookkeeping system must be zero. This kind of static, *a priori* constraint can be expressed as an *invariant*: a predicate on system states that must always be true. If a system state satisfies the invariant, the state is said to be *consistent*. If the system state always appears to be consistent, the system is said to be *internally consistent*.

While internal consistency is certainly desirable, it is not sufficient: not only should the system state be consistent, but the state should be a proper result of the history of external stimuli that have been presented to the system. For example, if the system is requested to perform some action and responds that the action has been done, then the system state should reflect the results of that action. That is, the system must be (internally) consistent and must also be consistent with external perceptions of its behavior. This latter property is called *external consistency*. External consistency is important because agents outside the system may act based upon system output; though the system may be able to undo internal actions, in general the effects of output cannot be undone. We will discuss this point more later. This discussion of consistency is based mainly on the following works: [EGLT76, Gray75, Gray78].

Because external consistency is not as familiar a concept as internal consistency, let us discuss it in more detail. Suppose that a user is interacting with the system via a terminal. A possible external consistency requirement is that once the system has typed *done* on the terminal in response to a request, then that request has actually been performed, in its entirety, and its effects are guaranteed not to disappear from the system (though of course later requests may modify data just written, etc.). We desire that the just stated external consistency property hold.[1]

More subtle external consistency properties involve the relative ordering of events in the system with respect to their output at the terminal. To simplify system design we might not require that actions be performed exactly in the order requested or in the order of the *done* messages printed on the terminal. This is especially true if many requests may be in progress at once. Further, if the requests perform their processing in different places, then it can be hard to tell which request was processed first, because the *done* messages may have taken varying times in transmission through the communications network. We require that if a new request is entered after the *done* message of a previous request has been printed, then the effects of the first request definitely precede the effects of the new request. Stronger ordering requirements, including relations between the output produced on different terminals, might be hard to achieve, and we do not require them. See [Lamport78] for further discussion of this issue.

In addition to being internally and externally consistent, the system should be *congruent*. That is, while failures may prevent the system from fulfilling some requests, or might even force the system to undo previously completed work, the system should attempt to act as closely as possible to what is requested of it. For example, the system should avoid spontaneous state transitions, even if it maintains external consistency by telling us what it does. Unlike consistency, which must be maintained for system correctness, congruity is a

---

1. But see the later discussion of input/output.

performance requirement and is difficult to formalize. Congruity might not be necessary for every application, but we will assume that the system is never to undo spontaneously (even in response to failure) anything it previously claimed was done. We also assume that the system initiates no spontaneous updates.

In sum, internal consistency is the requirement that the system state always (appear to) satisfy its invariant predicate. External consistency is the requirement that the system state correspond to external perceptions of it. Congruity is the further requirement that the system state reflect as closely as possible the correct response to external stimuli.

3.1.2 Actions.

Actions are the units of work performed by the system. Each action takes some input, possibly modifies the system state, and produces some output. In general, an action may be made up of other actions. An action and its sub-actions are related in a hierarchical fashion. As actions are broken down into smaller and smaller pieces, the eventual result is primitive actions. We will say more about primitive actions later. The primitive actions that make up a given action might not have to be executed sequentially - actions may exhibit internal concurrency. In this chapter we are concerned with actions consisting only of primitive actions. Hierarchical (nested) actions will be discussed in the next chapter.

A defining property of actions is that they preserve (internal and external) consistency. That is, each action, if executed in isolation and to completion, will leave the system in a consistent state if the system was in a consistent state to begin with. From now on it is *assumed* that the system is requested to perform only actions. That is, every request put to the system is assumed to preserve consistency (if executed in isolation and to completion).

It is not required that the system state be consistent in the middle of executing an action. It is often convenient, even essential, to violate consistency temporarily and restore it later. Note also that not every group of primitive actions will move the system from one consistent state to another. Actions are exactly those groups of primitive actions that do preserve consistency. Thus the notion of action arises naturally from the desire to maintain consistency of the system state.

3.1.3 Serializability.

Suppose the system is presented with a number of action requests. How might these requests be fulfilled without violating internal or external consistency? One simple method is to execute the requests one at a time. Such serial processing will preserve consistency in the absence of failures, because each action leaves a consistent state for the next action to act upon. Of course the initial state must also be consistent. A particular order of execution of the actions is called a *serial schedule*.

It is easy to see that serial schedules are correct (preserve consistency), but they can also lead to poor performance by not taking advantage of possible concurrency. On the other hand, arbitrary concurrency in the execution of actions can destroy consistency. Here is a simple example. Suppose two actions are to be performed; each of these actions increments a particular system variable. Further suppose that incrementing is performed by reading the current value of the variable, adding one to the value read, and storing the result back into the variable. If the two actions perform their reads before either action does the write back, then the effect will be as if the variable were incremented only once instead of twice. Moral: concurrency must be handled carefully.

To permit maximum concurrency while preserving consistency, we require that the system's execution of a group of actions be *equivalent* to some serial schedule of those actions. A schedule (i.e., a history of execution) is said to be *serializable* if it is equivalent to a serial schedule. The equivalence relation for schedules will be discussed below. Assuming the equivalence relation is correct (consistency preserving), serializability is sufficient for guaranteeing consistency in the face of concurrency. Note, though, that failures can still interfere with correct operation of the system. We will discuss failure in detail later in this chapter; for now it is assumed that failures do not occur.

3.2 Objects and Locking.

Two general methods have been used to achieve serializability: locking and timestamps. The design we present will use locking. However, we wish to emphasize that transactions (and nested transactions) are a *concept*, and can be divorced from particular implementation techniques. In both the locking and the timestamp method the system state is sub-divided into some number of non-overlapping *objects*. The locking method typically associates a *lock* with each object.[1] For an action to manipulate an object, the action must hold the object's lock. Only one action at a time may hold a given lock.[2] A further rule is that an action may not acquire (or re-acquire) any locks after it has released a lock. This is called the *two-phase locking* protocol (not to be confused with the two-phase *commit* protocol to be introduced later). In the first phase an action only acquires (does not release) locks, and in the second phase the action only releases (does not acquire) locks. Two-phase locking works because it insures that the order in which any two actions access the same object is the same as the order in which those actions access any other object. The underlying assumption is that if two schedules result in the same order of access at each object then the schedules are equivalent. Given the just stated equivalence relation on schedules, it is possible to prove that if the two-phase locking protocol is used then any actual schedule is equivalent to at least one serial schedule (see [EGLT76] for a proof). That is, two-phase locking insures serializability.

3.2.1 Read/Write Locking.

The kind of locks suggested above work fine. However, because reading is typically more common than writing, concurrency can be improved by distinguishing read and write access to objects and refining the locking scheme in the following way. A lock may be held for reading or for writing - these two cases are called *read mode* and *write mode* (hence the scheme is called read/write locking). If an action holds a write mode lock for an object, that

---

1. See [Gray78, Gray75] for a method that associates locks also with hierarchically organized groups of objects.
2. For now we are describing mutual exclusion locks. Read/write locking will be introduced a little later.

action is permitted to read the object as well as to write it. At most one action at a time may hold a lock in write mode; any number of actions may hold a lock in read mode concurrently. However, if an action holds a lock in write mode, then no other action may hold the lock in either mode. Here are the rules in detail:

Read/Write Locking Rules

- An action may acquire a lock in *read* mode if no other action holds the lock in *write* mode. If the action currently holds the lock in *read* or *write* mode, then the request has no effect: the action continues to hold the lock in the previous mode.
- An action may acquire a lock in *write* mode if no other action holds the lock in any mode. If the action currently holds the lock in *read* mode, it now holds it in *write* mode. If the action currently holds the lock in *write* mode, then it continues to hold the lock in *write* mode.
- An action must hold a lock in either *read* or *write* mode before reading the corresponding object.
- An action must hold a lock in *write* mode before writing or modifying the corresponding object.
- An action may not acquire (or re-acquire) any lock in any mode if it has released any locks.
- An action may release a lock it holds at any time.

The last rule will be modified later in this chapter. In [EGLT76] it is proved that two-phase locking guarantees serializability for read/write locks.[1] The proof is only slightly more subtle than with mutual exclusion locks. The key point is that the order of reads with respect to other reads is irrelevant: it is only the order of reads with respect to writes that matters.

Locking provides serialization on an object-by-object basis. This improves concurrency because most actions read or modify only small portions of the whole system state - that is, a

1. Actually, the previous citation of [EGLT76] was based on the fact that exclusion locking is just a special case of read/write locking (only write mode locks are requested).

typical action locks only a small fraction of the objects, and actions that lock other objects (or some of the same objects in non-conflicting modes) can proceed concurrently with no serialization. Just as consistency is part of the motivation for actions, concurrency is part of the motivation for splitting the system state into objects.

There is a natural trade-off between locking overhead (if there are many objects) and reduced concurrency (if there are few objects). The chosen granularity of objects controls this trade-off. In practice it has been found useful to vary the granularity of locks dynamically [Gray75] to get the effect of varying object granularity. Variable granularity is omitted from our design to maintain simplicity of locking and to avoid introducing the requisite embellishments to object structure. There is further discussion of variable granularity in Chapter 8.

The locking scheme we have suggested can result in deadlocks. Deadlock is discussed in detail in Chapter 6.

3.2.2 Choice of Primitive Actions.

We claimed that the refinement from exclusion locking to read/write locking improves concurrency. Indeed, it is generally the case that refinements to locking schemes based on improved semantic knowledge will enhance concurrency. Unfortunately, it is hard (if not impossible) for the system to acquire the necessary semantic knowledge automatically. For example, suppose a user implements a form of directories. Many, perhaps most, operations on a directory do not interfere with one another because they deal with separate entries in the directory. It seems unreasonable for the system to derive that fact from examination of the source code for directory management. We have taken a compromise position: all operations on objects are to be expressed (at the lowest level) in terms of reads and writes. Hence, the primitive actions of the system are reads and writes of individual objects. The system can certainly be built to "understand" the semantics of such a simple set of operations. Chapter 8 discusses some possible extensions.

The main objection to basing all locking on reads and writes is that in some cases further semantic knowledge would permit higher concurrency safely. A typical example is that of directories, mentioned above. Our answer to the objection is that some kind of loophole can be provided for suitably privileged or adventurous programmers to code important special cases that are not handled well by the automatic system we have suggested. We will not discuss the form such loopholes might take.

A second objection to our suggested locking scheme is that atomic actions are not always necessary. For example, when a user lists a directory, it might be all right to list files in the process of being created or destroyed. However, the user must understand that while the listing is informative, it is not entirely reliable because it may not represent a consistent view of the directory. There is no way the system can automatically detect cases where serializability is unnecessary, because the need for serialization is based upon the use of the output of an action. In the previous example, a user may be fully aware of the possible imprecision of a directory listing, but a program that is supposed to process all files in a directory probably requires a consistent view of the directory. We have chosen to insure safety of the system, though an implementation might provide loopholes for lower degrees of consistency. It is interesting to note, however, that although several degrees of consistency were proposed for System R [Gray75] and actually implemented, the conclusions of the designers was that only the highest degree (what we have called serializability) should be offered [Gray80b].

3.3 Tolerating Failures.

The preceding discussions have been conducted under the unreasonable assumption that failures do not occur. We now explain how actions behave if failures occur, and how to implement that behavior. Note that if consistency were the only concern, whenever a failure occurred we could set the system state to some simple (but internally consistent) value, and report that this has been done (to maintain external consistency). Congruity requirements capture our desire that failures should not erase effects that have been guaranteed to be permanent. So although the hard part of handling failure is insuring consistency, it is hard only because we simultaneously require congruity.

3.3.1 Failure Atomicity.

As we noted at the beginning of this chapter, if an action is interrupted in the middle, then there is no guarantee that the system state will be consistent. So, actions should be run to completion. However, instead of guaranteeing that actions are completed, we will insure a weaker but still sufficient property: that actions are performed entirely or not at all. This all-or-nothing property is called *failure atomicity*. A *transaction* is an action that exhibits failure atomicity (and abides by the locking protocols of the previous section). If a transaction is performed successfully, it is said to have *committed*; if a transaction is started but fails, then it is said to have *aborted.*

Why allow transactions to be aborted? There are two answers. First, a partially executed transaction that cannot continue because resources it requires are not available can indefinitely delay other transactions desiring resources held by the waiting transaction. Sometimes it is better to abort the waiting transaction so that the resources it holds can be freed and other transactions may proceed. In fact, should a deadlock arise among some transactions (each transaction is waiting for a resource held by the next), it is essential to abort at least one of the transactions engaged in the deadlock.

The second answer is that while an individual transaction may fail, a request that some action be performed can be implemented by repeatedly starting transactions to fulfill the request until one such transaction commits. Note the distinction between a *transaction request*, which is what is presented to the system by external agents, and a *transaction*, which is an instance of execution of a transaction request. Of course not every request can be fulfilled - a request might be meaningless or malformed in some way such that it can never be processed. Automatic resubmission of the request should be prevented in such cases.

Hence, it can be useful to distinguish between *errors*, which indicate transaction failure that will happen every time the transaction request is attempted, and *failures*, which are related only to accidents encountered by the particular attempt to fulfill the request. Typical examples of failures are node crashes and deadlocks. An example of an error is an unexpected (unhandled) overflow exception in the transaction code. Though we will sometimes distinguish failures from errors, we generally lump them together and use the term failure in a more generic sense. Automatic request retry is not included in our design - it is mostly irrelevant to our development (but see the discussion in the latter part of Chapter 6). A system implementor might add automatic retry where desired.

3.3.2 Object State Restoration.

Of the various failures to be tolerated (communications failures and node crashes), node crashes are the hardest to handle. When a node crashes, the volatile state disappears, which includes all intermediate state of transactions in progress at that node, i.e., everything not recorded in permanent storage.

Volatile memory is manipulated directly by transactions,[1] but permanent memory is not.[2] Hence, permanent memory must be updated periodically to reflect changes made to objects. Each object is represented by a combination of volatile and permanent storage. However, the permanent storage by itself must represent a consistent state of the objects stored at one node. So updates of permanent storage must be done carefully to insure that consistency is maintained. We will propose an automatic system for updating permanent memory. An advantage of the automatic system is that it insures updates are done in a correct fashion.

The real state of an object is whatever is recorded in permanent memory. Transactions manipulate a volatile memory copy, which is backed up to permanent storage at the appropriate time. It may be possible to omit volatile memory copies of objects that are not currently being used by any transaction. In that sense volatile memory forms a cache for permanent memory. It is possible and reasonable that the representations of objects on permanent and volatile storage are different; we trust that the transaction system will hide such differences from programs, which see only the volatile memory format. Anyway, we

---

1. Recall that volatile memory may include paging store and scratch files on secondary storage.
2. It might be possible to use some or all of permanent memory directly, but we do not assume so. Further, whether or not it is possible to use permanent memory directly, it is not a good idea to do so, because permanent memory must be updated carefully.

will not be particularly concerned with the details of object formats - we require that certain functionality be provided, but the techniques used to provide it do not matter.

The crucial piece of mechanism required is a way of *restoring* each (write) locked object to its previous state when (if) the transaction that locked the object aborts. There are two general methods for state restoration. The first one (which we call the *state* method) maintains two object states: the current state and the one in effect when the object was locked. This method is simple to implement - one just samples and saves the state of an object at the time it is first locked for writing by the transaction. The saved information is sufficient for restoring the object's state should the transaction abort.

In the other method one keeps the object's current state and a list of operations that must be performed to restore the object to its former state. We call this the *operations* method, since it records changes in terms of operations rather than states. The list of operations that will restore the object's state is called the *undo log*. Once a transaction commits or aborts, the undo logs for objects it locked may be discarded (after performing undo in the case of abort). See [Gray78, Gray79, Verhofstad78] for more detailed discussion of recovery techniques.

It should be noted that the incremental nature of the operations method is not what distinguishes it from the state method. The state method can be applied incrementally by recording only the changed parts of an object and their new values. The important difference is that the state method shows only what is different, whereas the operations method shows how. The operations method generalizes more readily than the state method: with an undo log we can roll the system backward and forward at will, even to intermediate points.

One might think that logs or sampled states are not really necessary, because the permanent memory copy of an object can be used to restore the object's state in case of transaction abort. However, restoring from the permanent copy is not sufficient to handle the extension of the transaction scheme of this chapter to the more sophisticated nested transaction scheme of the next chapter.

Should we use the state method, or the operations method? We choose the state method, because it is easily made automatic, and because it is easier to explain. The operations method is harder to automate because (in the general case, which is what we are discussing) it requires an *undo* procedure to be supplied for each update operation. Also (in the general case) these procedures must be provided by the programmer and cannot be constructed automatically. Not only do *undo* procedures present an increased programming burden, they can be subtle and will probably have more than their fair share of programming errors. The choice of state restoration techniques is discussed further in Chapter 8.

Note that there is not a fundamental difference between the state and operations methods: the state method is just a special case of the more general operations method (its operation is "restore this saved state"). At first it might appear that the operations method is inherently incremental (because it appends *undo* records to the log as the object is operated upon), and that state method is not (because the object state is sampled before the object is actually manipulated). However, the state method could be made incremental by recording each change to each memory cell performed by a transaction. This idea might not be so far-fetched given some hardware support; see [LGH80], for example.

Here is the state restoration method we suggest, in more detail. Each object is represented with a copy in volatile memory and one in permanent memory. When an object is locked for writing, its (volatile) state is sampled and saved so that it can be restored if necessary. The state sample may be kept in volatile memory; it need not be permanent because we have not yet touched the permanent copy of the object. Now we may manipulate the (volatile copy of the) object at will. Should it be necessary to abort the transaction that locked the object, we simply restore the former state of the volatile copy, and release the lock. We can discard the restoration information as soon as the object state has been restored. In the case of a crash, we restore the volatile version of the object from the permanent version; the effect is entirely equivalent to a transaction abort. Committing a transaction requires that we update the permanent memory copy of each object modified by the transaction. The individual writes to permanent memory must be performed atomically, as discussed in the previous chapter (however, see also the upcoming discussion of distributed commitment).

Since a transaction may abort at any time prior to commitment, we must hold transaction locks until the outcome of the transaction is certain. Otherwise we might reveal uncommitted updates. Also, we might not be able to re-obtain the locks necessary for undoing changes, or worse, the objects might have been updated again, etc. Therefore, we must follow not only the two-phase locking protocol, but also the additional rule that locks cannot be released until the transaction is committed or aborted.

While we have taken a particular position regarding transaction concurrency control and recovery, we would like to point out the existence of some alternative techniques. Rather than locking and holding transactions up when they desire a lock that is held, one can take a more *optimistic* approach to concurrency control. Transactions are permitted to run and read objects at will, making tentative updates in private buffers. At commit time, serializability checks are made. The advantage of optimistic concurrency control is that it can increase concurrency and throughput by eliminating bottlenecks and needless serialization. The potential disadvantage of the optimistic method is more work to redo, because conflicts are not discovered until a transaction has finished normal processing and attempt to commit. Thus, optimistic concurrency control's effectiveness depends on the relative likelihood of of transaction conflicts, which is application dependent. One paper on this topic is [KR81].

The concept of optimism can be applied in other ways, too. One can permit transaction to read uncommitted writes of other transactions. This will not violate serializability if there is no cycle of dependencies created. Again, the advantage is increased concurrency and the hope of higher throughput. The disadvantage is that should one transaction abort, all transactions depending on its results, directly or indirectly must be tracked down and aborted. This property has been called *cascading abort*. This approach may be seen in [Takagi79], for example.

While we have been discussing optimism and concurrency above, optimism is related to recovery and state restoration. Not only do the optimistic methods we have described depend on state restoration to resolve the supposedly unlikely conflicts or aborts, but optimism is directly relevant to recovery management. In fact, one is usually optimistic: we assume the system will probably keep working, and design for good performance in the normal case, rather than good performance in crash recovery. Going beyond the usual optimism is a topic of current research [SY84].

Our present development takes the more conservative, "pessimistic" approach. However, we do so not because we feel optimism is inferior, but primarily to keep the design simple and manageable. In many application domains optimism may indeed be of significant value, but we are not aware of significant testing of the concept. Below is a summary of our state restoration method.

State Restoration Method
(and modified locking rules)

- When a transaction first acquires a *write* lock for a given object, the state of the object is examined and sufficient information saved to restore that state later.
- When a transaction *aborts*, restore the saved states of all objects for which the transaction holds *write* locks, and then release all locks.
- When a transaction *commits*, update (in one atomic step) the permanent memory versions of all objects for which the transaction holds *write* locks, and then release all locks.
- A transaction may not release any locks except as specified in the preceding two rules.

The details of the commitment procedure are given below.

3.3.3 Reliable Distributed Commitment.

To abort or commit a transaction correctly, we must make sure that either all its updates are written to permanent memory or none of them, even when the updates may have been performed at a number of different nodes. There is a well-known[1] technique for achieving this end, called the *two-phase commit protocol*. We will first describe a simple version of this algorithm, and then briefly mention some fancier versions that have better properties.

---

1. See [Gray78], for example.

Keep in mind that the protocol is specifically designed to work even if crashes occur at any point in its execution. It is also designed to handle any of the communications failures admitted in the previous chapter.

At this point we note that each object resides entirely at a single node. Hence communications failures do not affect the locking and state restoration rules because those rules do not involve communication. Some people might object that we do not support distributed or replicated objects. However, it is simpler to provide such objects by building another layer on top of the transaction system. Chapters 7 and 8 also discuss replication.

Suppose that we have somehow decided that a given transaction should be committed (or aborted). The process of actually committing or aborting the transaction will be called *transaction resolution*. The nodes that have done work on behalf of the transaction that we wish to resolve are called the *participants*. Some node in the system (often, but not necessarily, one of the participants) is chosen to play a special role, the *coordinator*. The coordinator is the moving force, with the participants responding passively. Assuming we desire to commit transaction *t*, the coordinator performs the following algorithm:

1. Send the message *prepare* (*t*) to each participant.[1] The coordinator is now said to be *preparing* the transaction.

2. Await responses from the participants. If any participant responds *abort* (*t*), then the transaction must be aborted (go to step 5). If all participants respond *prepared* (*t*) then the transaction may be committed (go to step 3). If some participants do not respond within a chosen timeout period, one can either abort the transaction (go to step 5), or retransmit *prepare* messages to the participants that have not yet responded and continue to await their responses. Eventually one will proceed to either step 3 or step 5.

3. Record in permanent memory a list of the participants along with a notation that transaction *t* is now *completing*. Send the message *complete* (*t*) to each

1. The coordinator is considered to be distinct from the participant at the same node (if any). If there is a local participant, its message may be delivered in a different way and with higher probability of success, but that is irrelevant to the correctness of this algorithm.

participant.[2]

4. Await responses from each participant. They *must* respond *completed*. If there are some participants that have not responded after a timeout period, retransmit the *complete* message to those participants. Once all participants have responded, erase the list of participants and associated information from permanent memory. Done.

5. Send the message *abort* (*t*) to each participant. Done.

If there is a crash, then the coordinator may perform some actions on recovery. In particular, if there is a record of a completing transaction, then the coordinator uses the saved list of participants to resume the above algorithm at step 3. If there is no such record, then the transaction is either aborted, or has already completed.

The two phases of the algorithm should now be apparent: in the first phase (called the *prepare* phase) the coordinator attempts to get every participant prepared. In the second phase (the *complete* phase) the coordinator completes the transaction at all participants.

The participants act as follows:

- If a *prepare* (*t*) message is received, and *t* is unknown at the participant (it never ran there, was locally aborted, or was wiped out by a crash), then respond *abort* (*t*). Otherwise, locally prepare the transaction as follows. Write the identity and new state of any objects *write* locked by the transaction to permanent memory. However, the old state of the objects is *not* overwritten - the point is to have both the old and new state recorded in permanent memory, so that the transaction can be locally committed (by installing the new states) or aborted (by forgetting the new states) on demand, regardless of crashes. This write to permanent memory must be performed as a single atomic update (see the previous chapter for discussion of what that means). When a transaction is prepared, its *read* locks may be freed

---

2. It is more traditional to use the term *commit* where we have used *complete*. However, *complete* is more consistent with the terminology to be used in Chapter 5. Also, it is not unreasonable to say that the transaction has committed once it turns control over to the coordinator, for it is then committed to accepting whatever outcome the coordinator achieves for it.

immediately, but *write* locks must be held until the transaction is resolved. Once the transaction is locally prepared, send the message *prepared* (*t*) to the coordinator.

- If an *abort* (*t*) message is received, then locally abort *t*: if *t* is prepared, erase from permanent memory the potential new states of objects modified by it (use a single atomic write), and then perform the usual volatile state restoration and unlocking associated with transaction abort.
- If a *complete* (*t*) message is received, then *t* must have been locally prepared, and is either still prepared, or already completed. If it is prepared, install the tentative new states of objects modified by the transaction, in both permanent and volatile memory, discarding the old states of those objects. Naturally, the permanent memory update should be done as a single atomic write. Finish committing the transaction by releasing all its locks. If *t* is no longer locally prepared, then it has already been completed, and no special action is required. In either case (*t* is locally prepared or not), respond *completed* (*t*) when done.
- If a transaction has been prepared for a long time and nothing has been heard from the coordinator, then ask the coordinator the state of the transaction. The coordinator responds *prepare* (*t*) if the coordinator is still preparing, *complete* (*t*) if it is completing. If the coordinator is not running or there is no record of the transaction, then the node where the coordinator ran will respond *abort* (*t*).

If there is a crash at a participant, nothing special happens. If a transaction was prepared, it is still prepared, because the permanent memory contains the necessary information. (On recovery the participant should check for prepared transactions and set up the volatile memory data structures, such as locks, so that unresolved updates will not be visible to new transactions.) If a transaction was not yet prepared, then the crash will wipe it out, and the transaction will be aborted all other places later. If the transaction was already completed, then the crash has no effect on it, since its updates have already been incorporated into the permanent versions of objects.

Below are state diagrams for the coordinator and participants of a transaction:

Coordinator States:

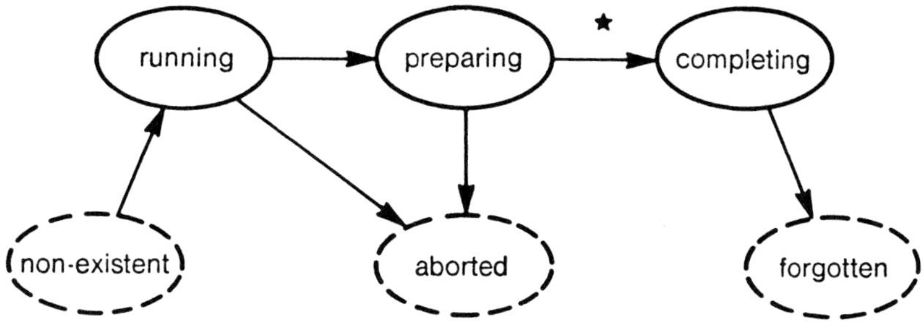

Participant States:

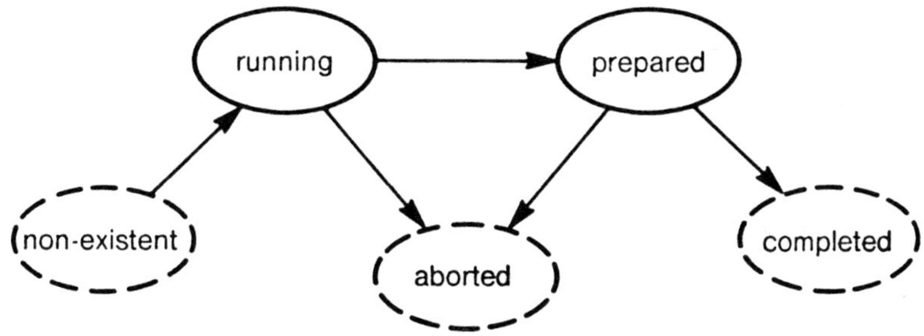

The states in the dashed enclosures are ones in which there is no record of the transaction at the node in question. In addition to the states discussed in the two-phase commit protocol, we show the earlier states of a transaction, from its creation. The starred state transition marks the "point of no return" - once that transition is taken the transaction is guaranteed to be completed. This will be argued below.

Let us now explore how and why two-phase commit works. First, we claim that if any participant *completes* the transaction, then all participants will complete it eventually. Reasoning backwards, if a participant completes, it can only be because it received a *complete* message from the coordinator. However, a participant will not receive a *complete* message unless the coordinator is completing the transaction. For the coordinator to be completing the transaction, *all* participants must have *prepared* the transaction. If a participant has prepared a transaction, then crashes will not affect that participant's data concerning the transaction. That is, once a transaction is prepared at a node, later it can be completed or aborted at will, and failures have no effect. Thus far we reason that if any participant completes a transaction, then all participants must have prepared the transaction. Note that it is important that participants respond *prepared* only after they have made the necessary writes to permanent memory. Also, it is important that the coordinator not make its record that it is completing the transaction until after all the participants have responded *prepared*.

The rest of the argument is this: once the coordinator starts completing, it is insured that every participant completes (responds *completed*) before the coordinator's data concerning the transaction is erased. So long as that data remains, crashes of the coordinator do not interfere with completion, because the coordinator starts completing again as soon as it recovers from a crash. The careful use of permanent storage helps give the algorithm immunity to crashes, and the retransmission of *complete* messages (in combination with querying of the coordinator by anxious participants) overcomes communications failures.

We have argued that if any participant completes, then all will complete eventually. Hence it is not possible for a transaction to complete at some participants and not others. So failure atomicity is guaranteed globally as well as locally. It should be easy to see that if the transaction aborts anywhere, it will eventually abort everywhere. This is true because the participants will query the coordinator, which will respond *abort*.

The last step in arguing correctness of two-phase commit is the claim that the algorithm eventually decides whether to commit or abort. Even without a timeout in step 2 of the coordinator algorithm, all participants will eventually respond, and the coordinator will decide whether to complete or abort.

There are two underlying assumptions here: that no nodes crash forever, and that eventually any given pair of nodes can communicate. The latter assumption is fairly reasonable; if necessary, certain messages could be spooled through third parties (see [HS80] for example). However, it is not quite so reasonable to assume that nodes may not fail permanently. We will return to this point in a moment.

There are some other facts to note about the algorithm. First, though it may seem slightly strange for a participant to respond *completed* when it receives a *complete* message for an unknown transaction, it is indeed correct. The situation arises when the first *completed* message is lost, or the coordinator crashes while completing. In any case, the participant must previously have prepared (or else it would not be asked to complete), so if there is no record, the transaction must already have completed.

Another point is that no special action (e.g., updating permanent memory) is required if the coordinator decides (or is forced) to abort. This is because a prepared participant will correctly assume that the transaction is aborted if the coordinator has forgotten about the transaction. Note that a prepared participant must wait for the coordinator to respond, however. If the coordinator is not responding (possibly because of a crash) it is possible that it has started completing, in which case the participant must complete; but it is also possible that the coordinator was aborting and the *abort* did not come through. A definite response is necessary to resolve the ambiguity.

The particular version of two-phase commit presented above is one of the simpler ones, but not necessarily one of the best. For one thing its efficiency is biased slightly towards the *abort* case rather than the *complete* case. Suitable reworking could make it so that the coordinator need only record the participants and persistently retransmit messages when the transaction is to be aborted. In fact, a number of adjustments are possible, under different assumptions; see [Gray80a] for example.

The main drawback of our simple two-phase commit protocol is that it is vulnerable to failure, in two senses:

- Permanent failure of the coordinator during the *complete* phase may cause some participants' never to resolve the transaction. The bad effect of this is that any objects updated by the transaction at those participants will remain locked forever. Even if the coordinator failure is not permanent, but just for a long time, this behavior can be intolerable in some applications.
- Permanent failure of a participant causes the coordinator to run forever. This is probably acceptable, provided some manual method is provided for getting rid of such coordinators once system administrators verify that the node in question will never again be available.

In [Reed78], Reed presents an algorithm that essentially replicates the coordinator and uses voting to decide whether to complete or abort. The key point is that completion does not require a unanimous vote, so we can avoid problems arising from any number of nodes being down by providing enough "copies" of the coordinator. Unfortunately, this commit algorithm is still vulnerable to failure of a single node at certain times. For example, suppose that the voting method used is three votes out of five decide the question (of whether to complete or abort). If two votes have been cast for completion and two for abortion, then the fifth "copy" is necessary to decide the question. If the fifth node fails at this time, the transaction will be unresolved until that node comes back up. While Reed's scheme narrows the window of failure considerably, it does not close it.

LeLann [LeLann81] presents a less elegant but more practical algorithm that permits transactions to be resolved if the coordinator fails; it requires that all participants be up. That is, LeLann's algorithm survives one node failure without hanging up, but not two failures. A more general approach to reliable distributed commitment is *Byzantine agreement*, so named from a coordination problem termed The Byzantine Generals by its inventors. A flurry of papers has been appearing on this subject. Our feeling is that Byzantine agreement is the ultimate in reliability, but indications are that it is relatively expensive, which may limit its use in practice. Some interesting papers on this topic are [BT83b, LSP82, LFF82, Schneider84].

However, it would not be difficult to substitute a different, more robust, version of two-phase commit or Byzantine agreement into our algorithms. Hence, we will use the simple version presented in this chapter to avoid needless complexity later.

Hammer and Shipman present a somewhat different approach to reliability of distributed processing in [HS80]. We will have more to say about it in Chapter 7.

3.4 Some Implementation Issues.

Up to this point we have not described in detail what objects and transactions look like or how they are manipulated. That was intentional: we do not wish to bias our work towards one particular implementation of objects. Also, it was important to introduce the necessary locking and state restoration concepts before discussing the issues further. However, at this point it seems useful to present one concrete alternative, though we do not intend to rule out other methods.

The simple object scheme we suggest is the following. At all times the state of an object is a string of bits, though the size of that string might vary and has no particular bound. Objects are identified by *object id*'s; the same object id can be used to find an object's volatile and permanent states. This implies that there is some method for translating object id's to both volatile memory addresses and permanent memory addresses. It also implies that object id's are unique, at least within a node. We will ignore issues in the translation of object id's to physical addresses, in the allocation of memory for object states, and in the construction of new object id's. Those issues present interesting and challenging problems, but are mostly orthogonal to this work.

Transactions are represented by *transaction id*'s. For simplicity we assume that transaction id's are unique (system wide), and never re-used (at least we will not investigate methods for reusing them safely).

The interesting operations of the scheme are ones to create, commit, and abort transactions (based on transaction id's), and to read and write the contents of objects as part of a given transaction. For safety and convenience, the locking, state restoration, and distributed commit functionality is built into the system, so the programmer need not follow special rules. However, if consistency is to be maintained, it is important that programs not communicate values read under a transaction until (and unless) that transaction has completed. A more complete design might provide means to insure that information flow that endangers consistency does not take place.

Here is a description of a possible set of operations. We stress that we are just trying to provide a simple example of how things might be done, and are not trying to design an actual implementation. A *tid* is a transaction id, and an *oid* is an object id.

create_transaction ( ) **returns** (*tid*)

> Returns a new (previously unused) transaction id.

commit_transaction (t: *tid*) **signals** (impossible)

> Attempts to commit *t*. This is *impossible* if *t* is foreign, aborted, or no longer known.

abort_transaction (t: *tid*) **signals** (impossible)

Attempts to abort *t*.

create_object (t: *tid*) **returns** (*oid*) **signals** (impossible)

Creates a new object and returns its id. The initial state of the object is the empty bit string. As with all manipulations of objects, creation is performed with respect to a given transaction (*t* in this case). The object is not definitely created until the transaction completes. If the transaction aborts, then it is as if the object never existed (except perhaps that the id might not be reused). Creating an object implies possession of a *write* lock on it. Implementation of object creation and deletion is discussed in Chapter 4.

delete_object (o: *oid*, t: *tid*) **signals** (impossible, nonexistent)

Deletes the indicated object. Deletion is not permanent until and unless *t* completes. A *write* lock is acquired on the object. The exception *nonexistent* is signalled upon any attempt to manipulate a deleted object.

read_object (o: *oid*, t: *tid*) **returns** (bits) **signals** (impossible, nonexistent)

Returns the current state of the object identified by *o*. A *read* lock is acquired on the object.

write_object (o: *oid*, b: bits, t: *tid*) **signals** (impossible, nonexistent)

Analogous to *read_object*, except that it sets the state of the object and acquires a *write* lock instead of a *read* lock

update_object (o: *oid*, t: *tid*) **signals** (impossible, nonexistent)

Acquires a *write* lock on the object without actually writing it. This is useful if a number of reads may be performed before writing, but it is desired to insure that writing will be possible later.

In all cases where locks must be acquired, operations either acquire the lock and succeed, or wait for the lock. That is, if a lock cannot be acquired, we assume that the requesting transaction is eventually aborted - the object operations do not signal an exception when a lock cannot be obtained.

The scheme just presented is simple partly because bit strings are very simple. If one desired to provide objects with more structure, then some subtle problems might arise. For example, if objects may have pointers inside them, it must be the case that pointers inside different objects never refer to the same storage - if they did, then the states of the objects would not be disjoint and the locking rules would not then insure consistent results. On the other hand, it is certainly permissible to store object id's in objects. Although object id's are pointers in a logical sense, access to the data referred to by them is controlled by the operations on objects, which perform the necessary locking.

We have been suggesting a class of implementations in which access to objects is mediated automatically, and it is therefore insured that the correct locking and state restoration actions are performed, in a correct way. One could certainly provide locks explicitly, along with a package of routines for doing locking and state restoration, where the routines are invoked by user code explicitly, rather than implicitly and automatically. Such schemes might be easier to retrofit to existing system and programming languages precisely because they are not integrated into the fundamental semantics and interface presented to the user. However, schemes requiring explicit user intervention are more tedious to use and less safe.

A last point: although it would be useful to have a more explicit model of the organization of user code and communication, we have chosen not to devise such a model. The main reason is that there is no general agreement on appropriate models for distributed computing, and we did not wish to bias our presentation towards any particular view. A second reason is that while a model of user computation might be convenient in discussing our system, it turns out not to be necessary. Hence, we present a somewhat "raw" interface, and it would be desirable to build a coherent user system on top of it. There is further discussion of this point in Chapter 8.

3.5 Recovery at the System Interface.

Just as updates to objects cannot be irrevocably performed until a transaction completes, neither can output be released. This congruity requirement, that output be produced if and only if the producing transaction completes, cannot always be met. The problem is that in general we cannot tell whether we have performed the output if a crash or similar failure occurs at a bad time. Within the system this is not a problem, because memory writes are idempotent: updating two or more times is equivalent to updating once.

Unfortunately, many output operations are not idempotent. A typical example is printing checks. If we print a check twice, then unless some external agent detects and suppresses the duplicate, we may very well end up paying the item twice, even though our records will indicate we paid it only once. Similarly, we wish to avoid printing the checks until the transaction completes, for otherwise we might pay an item and have no record.

There are two ways to deal with such problems. In cases where doing the output twice is not overly harmful, we can simply redo it. A typical example of such a case is a normal line printer listing; the only bad effect of producing a listing two or more times is wasted paper. Printing checks falls into the other category: if we err, we should err on the side of omitting some checks. Further, we should alert the operators that a crash happened at a delicate time, and the output should be examined so that the system can be issued further instructions to *compensate* for the failure. Compensation is distinguished from recovery in that recovery (e.g., state restoration) is handled entirely *within* the system and happens *automatically*, whereas compensation requires external interaction. Typically, though not always, the system consists of automatic machines, and compensation comes from human operators. If we extend the boundaries of the system, compensation can become recovery. However, unless the system includes the entire universe (unreasonable), then we will always reach a point where compensation will be required after completion. And not everything can be compensated (before you detonate a bomb, you had better be sure you want it to explode!) These comments are included to point out that even if we have a perfect recovery system, there remain some fundamentally insoluble problems.[1]

3.6 Summary.

In this chapter we have introduced the principles of consistency and congruity. We have suggested transactions and objects as abstractions to be supported by the system, and argued that serializability and failure atomicity are sufficient to obtain consistency and congruity in the face of the types of system failures admitted. We have proposed two-phase

---

1. The earliest statement of these ideas in similar form seems to be [Davies73].

locking as a technique for achieving serializability, and we have described a state restoration method that can be used to provide failure atomicity, if used in conjunction with the two-phase commit protocol for distributed transactions.

We have imposed considerably more structure on the system through the introduction of transactions and objects. We gave a very simple example of a set of operations for manipulating transactions and objects. Operations for communication (e.g., message passing) were not discussed, because we are not dealing with that aspect of the system in detail. Presumably *tid*'s may be sent from node to node so that a transaction may have work done on its behalf in different places.

This chapter has dealt with the concepts and general algorithms of traditional transaction processing. The next three chapters extend these concepts from the current single-level transactions to nested transactions. Chapter 4 describes the concept and semantics of nested transactions and extends some of the algorithms. Chapter 5 presents the extensions necessary because of the distributed nature of the system. Chapter 6 considers deadlock and the issue of progress in the system.

4. Subtransactions.

In the previous chapter the notion of *transactions* was presented, along with the general techniques that will be used to achieve consistency and congruity in our design. In this chapter, we extend the transaction idea by introducing *nested transactions* (also referred to as *subtransactions*). Our goal is to present the new locking and state restoration algorithms for nested transactions. However, first we must explain what nested transactions *are*. An actual design of a transaction manager, which incorporates a nested transaction distributed commit protocol, is presented in the next chapter.

4.1 What are Subtransactions?

Transactions are very useful and help solve many problems in both centralized and distributed computing. However, there are several problems remaining that are partially solved by adding subtransactions. The first problem has to do with modularity: difficulties arise when composing two or more previously written transaction routines into a single new transaction routine. (We use the term *transaction routine* to indicate the code executed when a transaction is run.) Suppose we write transaction routines in the following general way:

```
a_trans = proc (t: tid)
   ... actions with respect to t ...
   end a_trans
```

When we wish to execute the transaction, we write a simple program:

```
t: tid := create_transaction ();
a_trans (t);
commit (t);
```

If there were two existing transaction routines, *a_trans* and *b_trans*, that we wished to compose, we might do it this way:

```
t: tid := create_transaction ();
a_trans (t);
b_trans (t);
commit (t);
```

Hence it is not particularly difficult to compose transaction routines in the purely mechanical sense of gluing them together into a single transaction. However, if we can specify that *a_trans* and *b_trans* be executed concurrently instead of serially, then serious problems result. Specifically, if the two transaction routines manipulate some of the same objects, we can get unexpected, non-serializable behavior, just as if we ran two transactions without appropriate locking. That is, even if each of *a_trans* and *b_trans* always produces consistent results when run alone, there is no guarantee that their concurrent composition will insure consistency.

To allow easy composition of transaction routines, we should run the composition as a transaction in its own right, but also provide concurrency control *within* the transaction. The natural method is to consider the whole transaction as a microcosm and synchronize its components (called its subtransactions) with respect to each other in the way whole transactions are synchronized. This results in two levels of transactions: *top-level* transactions, the kind of transactions discussed in the previous chapter; and subtransactions, the separate pieces composed to make new composite top-level transactions. Once we admit two levels, it is natural to generalize to a hierarchy, so that we may compose transaction routines that are themselves compositions. The result is a structure with nested worlds of synchronization.

Safe concurrency within transactions, as just discussed, is not the strongest advantage of nested transactions. While intra-transaction concurrency can be useful, especially in a distributed system, where more than one processor can support a single transaction, it does not change the meaning of transactions, but only offers improved performance. On the other hand, the finer grained recovery possible with nested transactions significantly extends the semantics of the transaction model, and in quite useful ways.

For example, suppose we wish to perform a distributed transaction, consisting of several subtransactions each doing something at a different node. As we increase the number of nodes, or the duration of the transaction, the probability of failure increases, such that in the limit the top-level transaction's probability of success goes to zero.[1] However, if we treat subtransactions as full-fledged transactions within the microcosm of their containing transaction, then failure of one of the subtransactions need not affect the outcome of any others. Of course, if the application requires that *all* nodes perform the requested action, then a failed subtransaction must be retried until it succeeds. The point is that only the failed subtransactions need be redone. Thus each subtransaction (at any nesting level) acts like a firewall, preventing outside influences from affecting the internals. Also, each transaction partly shields the outside world from failures inside the transaction. If the independent failure property of subtransactions is coupled with appropriately timed writes to permanent storage (so the effects of a completed subtransaction are not lost in a later crash), then we might be able to raise the limiting probability of success from zero to one. This aspect of subtransactions will be discussed in more detail later.

When a subtransaction completes successfully, it will be said to have *committed*, even though it is not a top-level transaction. Of course, such commitment is relative: any updates become permanent only if all the subtransactions containing the committed subtransaction also commit, and the enclosing top-level transaction completes. Thus, top-level transactions are special: they are the only irrevocable transactions. Similarly, we will also speak of an unsuccessful subtransaction as having *aborted*, though, as we pointed out above, this does not imply that any of the containing (sub)transactions must abort. Aborting is always irrevocable in the sense that an aborted transaction's work must be undone. The details of the relationship of committing and aborting of subtransactions to committing and aborting of their containing transactions, including the manipulation of locks and state restoration information, form the bulk of this chapter.

---

1. This does not mean that the transaction cannot succeed; just that it is infinitely more *likely* to fail than succeed.

4.2 Some Terminology.

Before proceeding to the details of synchronization and recovery of nested transactions, it is useful to introduce some terminology. First, we will use the term *transaction* to include both top-level transactions and nested transactions (subtransactions). Now we define some more terms using the diagram below:

A Transaction Nesting Diagram

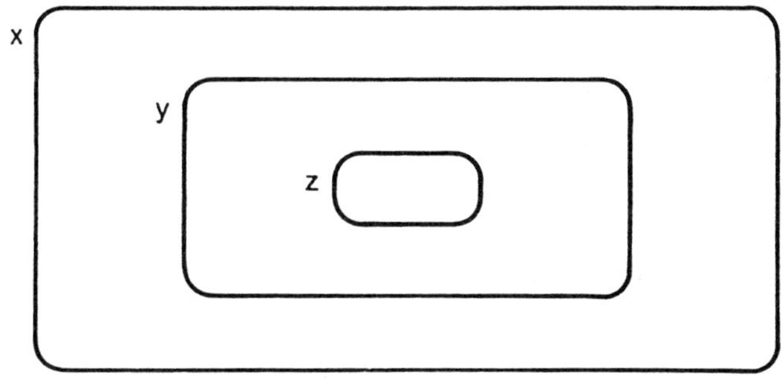

The diagram illustrates three transactions, *x*, *y*, and *z*. The contours[1] indicate that *x* has greater scope than *y*, that is, that *y* is a subtransaction of *x*. Likewise *z* is a subtransaction of *y*. The contours emphasize the idea that each transaction is a miniature universe of synchronization and recovery. Contours will never intersect, because a subtransaction's world and lifetime are always strictly bounded by those of its containing transaction (if any). We will often find it convenient to describe transaction relationships using trees instead of nested contours.[2] Here is the tree corresponding to the preceding diagram:

---

1. Our figures were inspired by Davies' [Davies73] diagrams and his term *spheres of control*.
2. The two forms of description are equivalent because each encodes hierarchical relationships, which are the relationships of interest here.

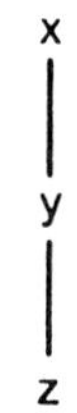

If we had two top-level transactions, *x* and *x*', each with a subtransaction, the situation could be drawn this way:

If *x* had two subtransactions either of these diagrams would describe the situation:

Tree Diagram

Nesting Diagram

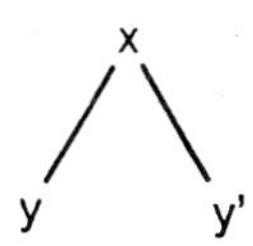

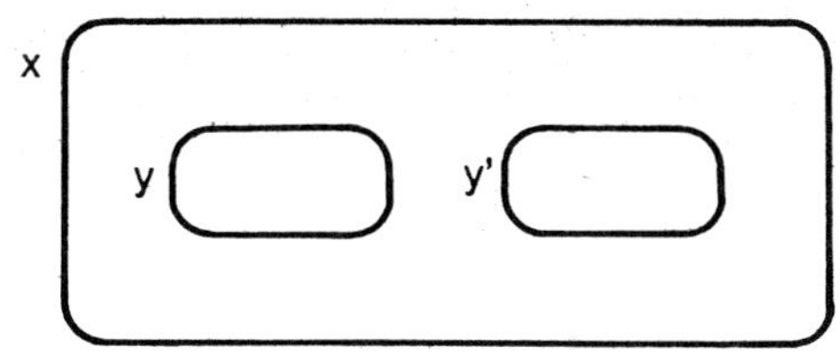

Note that the lifetimes of *y* and *y*' might overlap or they might not - the diagrams do not say. Fortunately it almost never makes a difference because the locking rules we present later will prevent any ill effects from concurrent execution.

Because transaction relationships follow trees, we will often use tree terminology, or terms for familial relationships, to express transaction relations. Thus, transactions having no subtransactions may be called *leaf* transactions. Transactions having subtransactions may be called *parents*, and their subtransactions are their *children*. Similarly, we will speak of *ancestors* and *descendants*. It will be convenient to say that a transaction is an ancestor and descendant of itself (i.e., the ancestor and descendant relations are reflexive). We will use the terms *superior* (*inferior*) for the non-reflexive version of *ancestor* (*descendant*). Because the distinction between ancestor and superior is often important, we have been careful always to use the terms in the technical sense just described.

4.3 Synchronizing Nested Transactions.

Let us first consider exclusion locking for nested transactions, and make the extension to read/write locking later. This will simplify the initial presentation.

In the simplest case, where nested transactions arise only by composition of previously written one-level transaction routines, all manipulation of objects is performed by the leaf transactions. Parent transactions perform only coordination and supervisory functions and could be said (metaphorically) to live vicariously through their children. What is the correct locking scheme in this simple case?

For synchronization of leaf transactions with each other, the traditional and obvious rules suffice: if a lock is granted, then the locking transaction has exclusive access to the locked object until the transaction commits or aborts, and no other transaction can lock the object for that period of time. However, we need additional mechanism and rules to handle some cases. Here is a little example. Suppose we have some transactions related as in this nesting diagram:

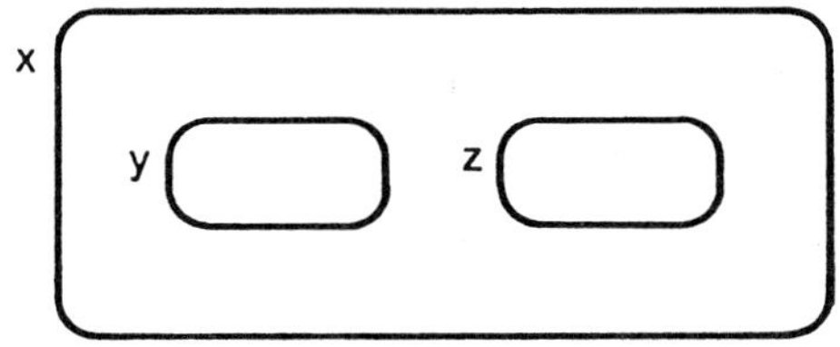

Further suppose that *y* and *z* are processed serially and both lock the same object. (There is no conflict because the transactions' lifetimes do not overlap.)

A first observation is that when *y* commits, the lock cannot be entirely released. The reason is that *x* can still abort, undoing *y*'s changes. So, to insure serializability, we must make sure that transactions "outside" of *x* (i.e., not within *x*'s microcosmic universe) cannot see the changes until *x* commits. The solution is to "move" the lock from *y* to *x* when *y* commits, thus showing that nothing outside of *x* can lock the object. At this point there is a complication in that we would like to permit *z* to acquire the lock, but we said that *x* inherited the lock from *y*. The problem is only conceptual, and there are several ways out of it. We choose the following way because it is simplest. However, see the corresponding section of [Moss81] for a slightly different technique.

We restrict non-leaf transactions to perform no primitive operations on objects directly. Rather, only leaf transactions will directly manipulate objects. Note that should one desire a parent to perform a primitive, one need only introduce a new child to perform the action on the parent's behalf. (The new child is a leaf transaction.) Our restriction does not significantly reduce the generality of the model, and special techniques could be employed in an actual implementation to avoid the overhead of the additional level of nesting. In sum, leaf transaction directly manipulate objects, and non-leaf transactions do not.

When a transaction commits, its parent will *inherit* the committing child's locks. The inherited lock is a place holder indicating that transactions outside the holder's universe cannot acquire the lock, but inferior transactions (ones inside the holder's universe) can. Figure 1 shows the sequence of situations as *y*, then *z*, and lastly *x* run and commit.

There is a detail yet to be settled: we have said what to do if an inferior commits, but what if it aborts? We could either just release its locks, or we could have its parent inherit them. Why would we ever want the parent to inherit a lock, since the transaction aborted, and therefore could not have had any effect on permanent storage? The difficulty is that the aborted transaction may have communicated information outside (e.g., to its parent). This problem was present in the single level transaction system of the previous chapter. There we explained how we must assume that transactions do not irrevocably communicate information outside of themselves unless and until they commit, for otherwise external consistency is endangered.[1] The reason the situation is worse now is that if an inferior

1. We also explained how we could not assume that communication to the outside world was always perfect, but that is not the point here.

Figure 1. Example of Lock Inheritance.

① Transaction *x* is running.

② *x* creates an inferior, *y*.

③ *y* acquires the lock, and holds it.

④ *y* has committed, so *x* *inherits* the lock.

⑤ *x* creates another inferior, *z*.

⑥ *z* acquires the lock, and *holds* it. This is permitted because *z* is inferior to the only holder of the lock, *x*.

⑦ *z* has committed, and *x* still holds the lock. There is no need for a concept of holding a lock "two times", or more.

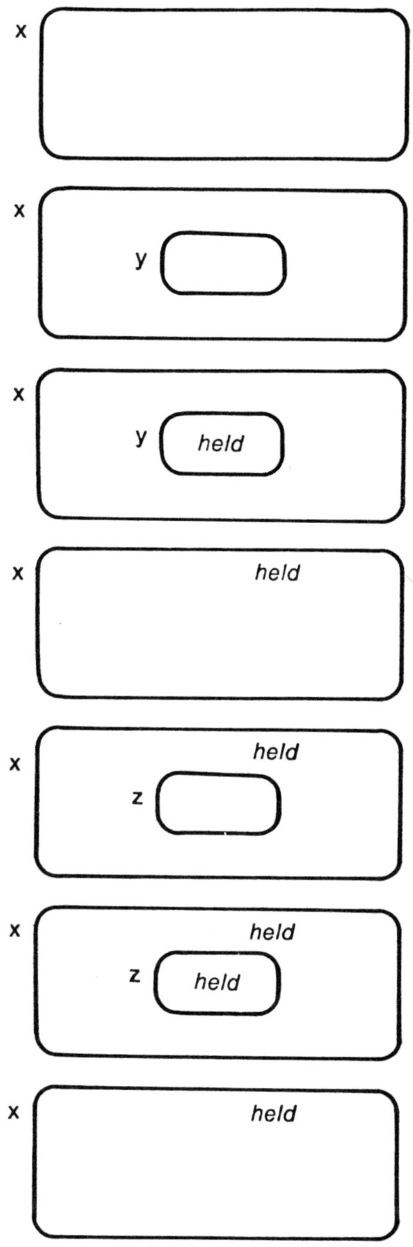

aborts because of an error[1], it is reasonable to provide at least *some* information to the parent about why the child could not proceed. If we provide more than minimal information (e.g., if we permit the user's code to return an error message of some kind), then consistency might possibly be violated, provided the parent acts on the information improperly. A reasonable approach is to inherit locks if a child is in error, but to release locks otherwise. In either case, any updates the child made to objects should be undone. However, since our design will omit special handling of transaction errors (as opposed to failures), locks will be discarded upon transaction abort.

It is useful to release locks in the failure case. If deadlocks are resolved by aborting transactions, then less work will have to be redone after a deadlock is broken. The reason is that if locks of aborted transactions are inherited, then we must always abort entire top-level transactions to break deadlocks, but if the locks are simply discarded we can be less heavy-handed in aborting transactions to extricate ourselves from deadlocks. Deadlock is discussed in more detail in Chapter 6.

Here are the locking rules for our simple case. The rules are more general than necessary for this case, so that they will be more easily extended later.

Initial Locking Rules

- A transaction may hold a lock if all other holders of the lock are superiors of the requesting transaction.
- When a transaction commits, its parent (if any) inherits all locks the inferior held.
- When a transaction aborts, all locks it holds are discarded (released). If any superiors of the aborted transaction hold the lock they continue to do so.

The above rules assume that a transaction does not commit until all its inferiors have terminated (so that it inherits any necessary locks, and passes them on to its parent). Note,

---

1. Recall that an error is a situation that a transaction routine is not prepared to handle. Errors are distinguished from failures, which are accidents (such as crashes and deadlocks) that might not reoccur if the transaction is run again.

though, that the semantics of nested transactions specify that the lifetime of a child is always contained in its parent's lifetime. Hence the required commit order is insured. We will see in the next chapter that it requires some effort to commit transactions in the correct order, but it is necessary if we are to support nested transaction semantics properly.

A possible objection to the simple model presented above is that prohibiting parent transactions from directly accessing objects is unnecessarily restrictive, unnatural, or inefficient (assuming that creating and manipulating inferior transactions has significant cost). It is easy to relax the restriction and permit parents to manipulate objects. However, some problems arise.

What should happen if a transaction and one of its inferiors request concurrent access to the same object? If the inferior locked the object first, the superior could just wait for the inferior to complete and free up the object, or possibly abort the inferior if the superior becomes impatient. However, if the superior locked the object first, the inferior cannot possibly be granted the lock, since the lock will be held until the end of the superior transaction. So, the inferior might as well be aborted right away. The situation just described is actually a deadlock between the superior and inferior transactions. The algorithms of Chapter 6 will deal with such situations.

There are alternatives to the above approach to the problem of concurrent access by superiors and inferiors. For example, it would be reasonable to say that any concurrent access by a superior and an inferior is incorrect, and rule it out. One could also just assume that the programmer is doing the right thing and permit the concurrent access, though this approach seems dangerous. We will stick with the approach first stated because it is safe. However, our design could readily accommodate different decisions about concurrent access by superiors and inferiors.

Now we extend synchronization to provide *read* and *write* mode locking. This is most easily explained by just stating the

Final Locking Rules

- A transaction may hold a lock in *write* mode if all other transactions holding the lock (in any mode) are superiors of the requesting transaction.
- A transaction may hold a lock in *read* mode if all transactions holding the lock in *write* mode are superiors of the requesting transaction.
- When a transaction aborts, all its locks, both *read* and *write*, are simply discarded. If any of its superiors hold the same lock, they continue to do so, in the same mode as before the abort.
- When a transaction commits, all its locks, both *read* and *write*, are inherited by its parent (if any). This means the parent holds each of the locks, in the same mode as the child held them.

In the last rule we must perform a "union" (least upper bound) of some lock modes. The basic modes are *none* (the lock is not possessed at all), *read*, and *write*. These modes are ordered:

$$none < read < write$$

Using that ordering, it is easy to describe how a parent's new mode is set when a child commits:

parent's new mode = max (parent's old mode, child's mode)

A transaction's mode obeys the rule that the mode never decreases. Thus, whenever a transaction requests and is granted a lock, it holds the lock in the maximum of the requested mode and the mode in which it previously held the lock:

new mode = max (requested mode, old mode)

For simplicity, most of the examples presented showed sequential subtransactions. However, the locking rules work for concurrent subtransactions - in fact, concurrency is one of the reasons for locking in the first place. While we will not present a proof of the locking rules, here is a sketch of a correctness argument. First, holding a *write* lock prevents any other transaction from accessing the locked object, and holding a *read* lock prevents the object from being written. Next, inheritance of *write* locks when a transaction commits has two effects: it permits transactions *within* the parent's microcosm (i.e., inferiors of the parent) to see any changes, and to make further updates; and it prevents transactions outside the microcosm from either reading or writing the object. Inheritance of *read* locks when a transaction commits prevents updates by transactions outside the parent's microcosm. This insures that the parent's world is presented with a consistent snapshot of the objects it manipulates. A proof of our rules may be found in [Lynch83].

As in the previous chapter, we leave unspecified what happens in case a requested lock cannot be granted, deferring discussion of deadlock issues to Chapter 6.

4.4 State Restoration.

As was the case with locking, we need to extend our previous ideas about object state restoration when we proceed from single-level transactions to the nested transaction scheme. Before we had an "old" state and a "new" or "current" state of each object locked for writing. A simple example will illustrate that two object states are no longer always sufficient. Consider this transaction nesting diagram:

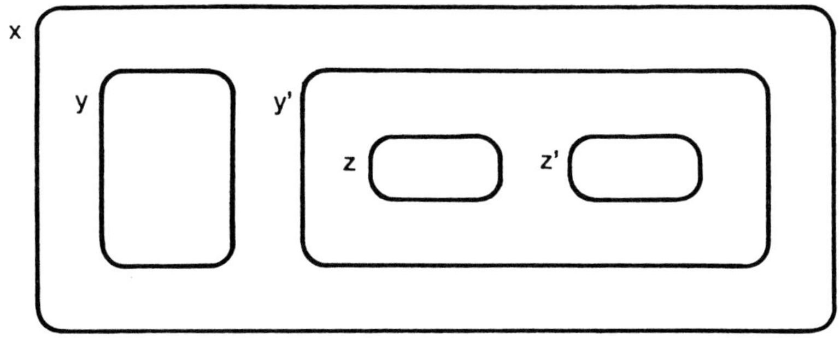

Suppose that *y*, *z*, and *z'* all modify the same object, that *y* and *z* have committed, and we are now at the end of *z'*. If *z'*, *y'* and *x* commit, then we should install the current state of the object. If *z'* aborts, then we need to restore the state of the object as it was before *z'* but after *y* and *z*. If *y'* aborts, then we need to restore the state pertaining after *y* and before *z* or *z*'. Lastly, if *x* aborts, then we need to restore the state pertaining before *x*.

Instead of having just an "old" and "new" state, it is easy to see that we need to represent the current state, and for each unfinished transaction that modified the object (directly, or indirectly through descendants), the state that should be restored if that transaction aborts. In the above example, we need the current state, the state to restore if *z*' aborts, the one to restore if *y*' aborts, and lastly the one to restore if *x* aborts.

We can use our former methods for sampling the state of the object. However, there was an optimization we mentioned in the previous chapter that cannot be used here except in one special case. Before, we could omit actually sampling the state of the object because the copy in permanent memory was sufficient; that is, we could use the permanent memory copy to restore an object's state in case of an abort. In the above example, that trick can still be used in case transaction *x* aborts, but it does not apply to *y*' or *z*'. For simplicity of description, we will omit this optimization, though it might be used in an actual system.

4.4.1 State Restoration Algorithm.

Let us defer for a moment considerations of whether the various states of an object reside in permanent or volatile storage, and concentrate on the state restoration algorithm in general. First, we find it easiest to think of the object itself as always possessing the current state, with the information for restoring its state to previous values being separate and possibly of a different format. Doing state restoration in this way makes the mechanism more transparent to the user, because the user will see only the current version of the object at any time and does not have to be aware of or manage multiple versions of objects.

Restoration involves using previously saved restoration information to modify the current state so that it becomes the desired previous state. It turns out that we need restoration information for a given object for each transaction that holds a *write* lock on the object, for these are the only transactions which need to undo any modifications to the object. Further, the restoration information associated with a given object and transaction should be sufficient to restore the object to the state it had just prior to the first time the transaction locked the object for writing. These requirements form the basis of the following state restoration algorithm.

With each holder of a *write* lock on an object we connect some state restoration information for that object, called an *associated state* (for the given object and transaction). Associated states are created and manipulated as follows:

- When a transaction starts to hold a *write* lock on an object, the object is examined and restoration information sufficient to restore its current state is created and becomes the associated state for that object and transaction. This is done only if there is not already an associated state for the same object and transaction. An associated state might already exist if one of the transaction's children (directly or indirectly) modified the object and committed; see the other rules.
- When a transaction aborts, each of its associated states is used to restore the objects directly or indirectly modified by the transaction. Those associated states can then be discarded.
- When a transaction commits, each of its associated states is offered to the committing transaction's parent. The parent accepts each state (making it the parent's own associated state for the same object) if and only if the parent does not already have an associated state for the same object. Thus, if the parent does not have an associated state for one of the objects, then the associated state will not be lost, and the object will be correctly restored in case of later abort. However if the parent already has an associated state for the object, then the one the parent has should take precedence, because the parent's is earlier than the child's.

Perhaps it would be helpful to go through the various steps for the transactions previously illustrated (x, y, y', z, and z'). Figure 2 presents a series of snapshots showing the creation and inheritance of associated states. We represent an associated state for a given object and transaction by writing the object name and the associated state value in a box attached to the transaction's contour in the diagram.

It should be noted that this state restoration algorithm assumes that each of a transaction's inferiors is finished (committed or aborted) before the transaction itself may commit or abort. Otherwise, the associated states are not inherited and discarded properly. As mentioned before, the proper termination order must (and will) be guaranteed.

Figure 2. State Restoration Example.

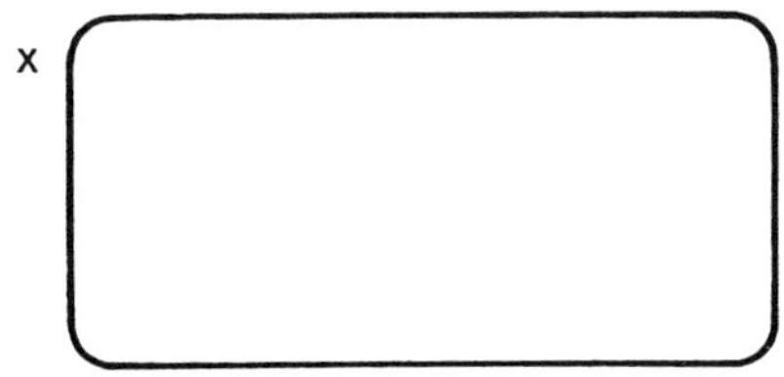

① *x* was just created.

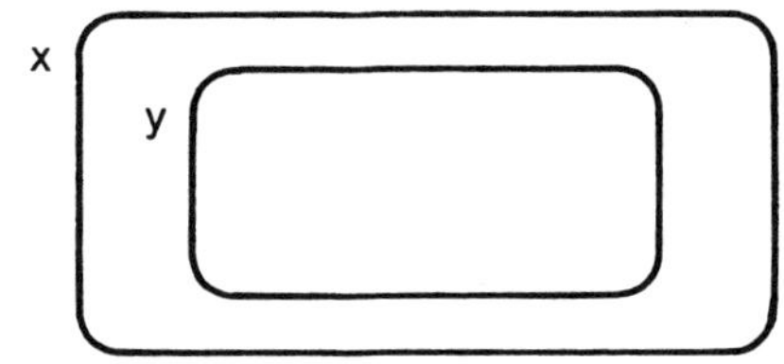

② *y* has started.

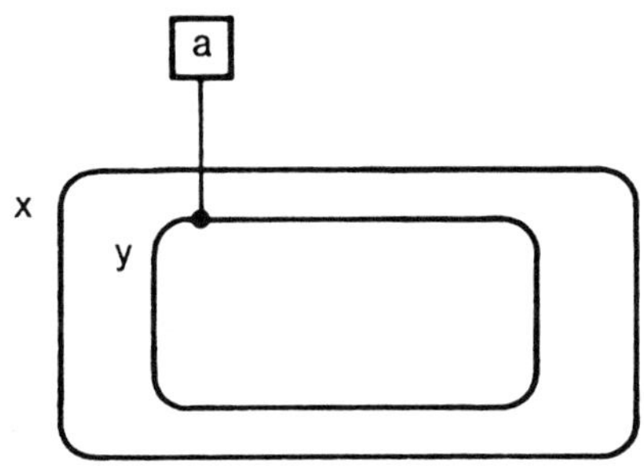

③ *y* has locked the object, causing associated state *a* to be created.

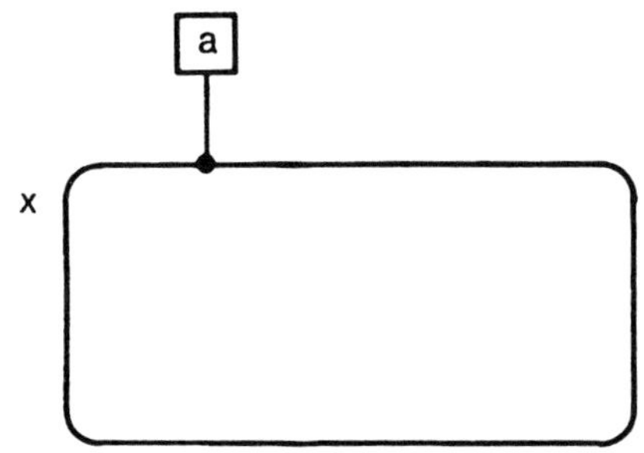

④ *y* has committed, and *x* has inherited the associated state ***a***.

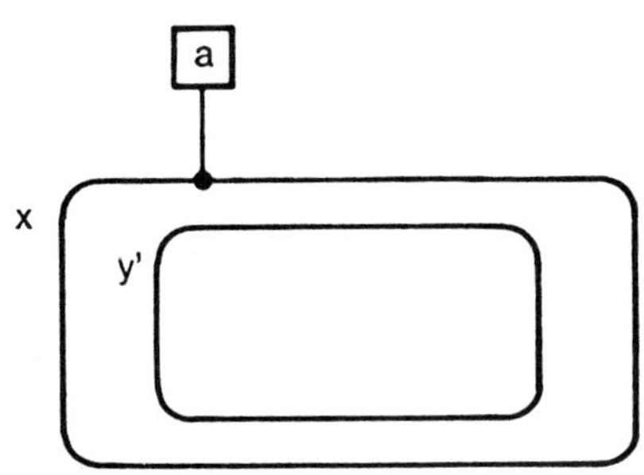

⑤ *y'* has been created.

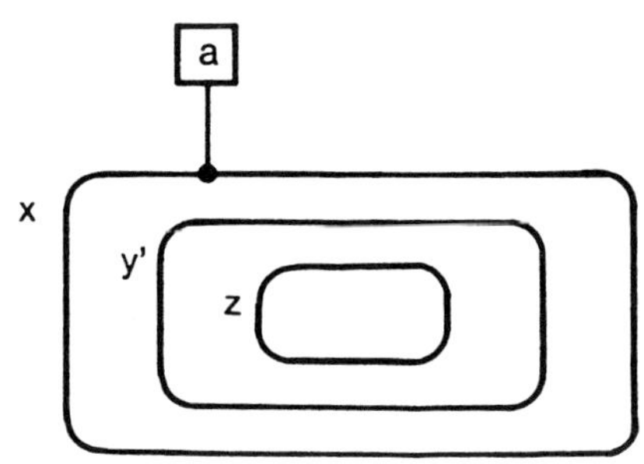

⑥ *y'* has created ***z***.

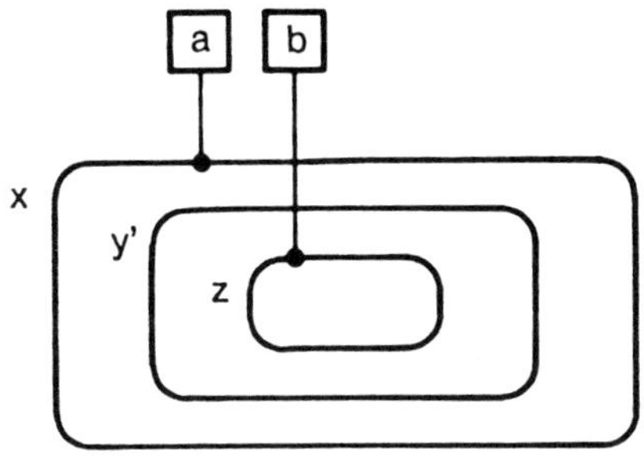

(7) *z* has locked the object for writing, causing associated state *b* to be created.

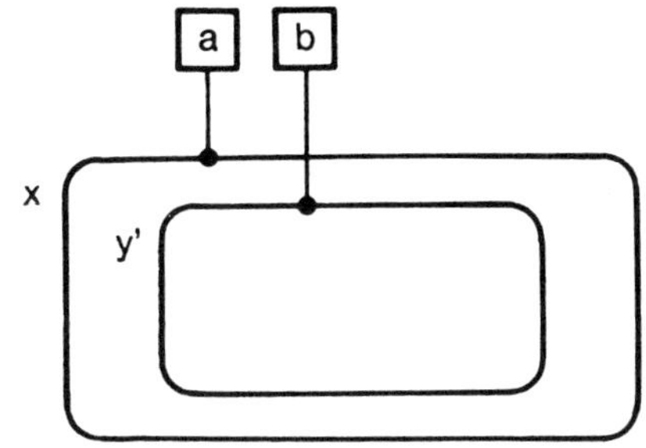

(8) *z* has committed, and *y*' has inherited associated state ***b***.

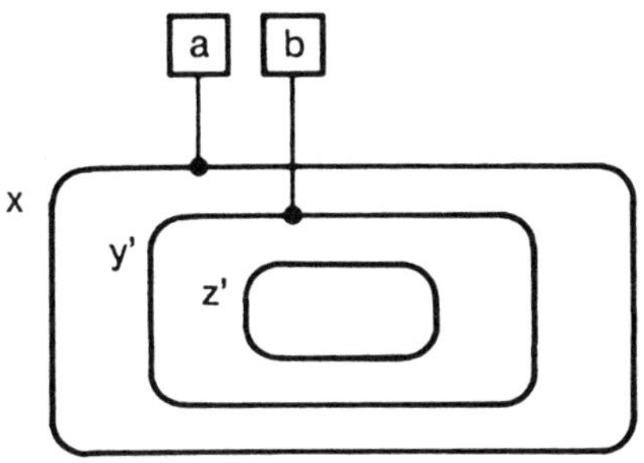

(9) *y*' has created ***z*'**.

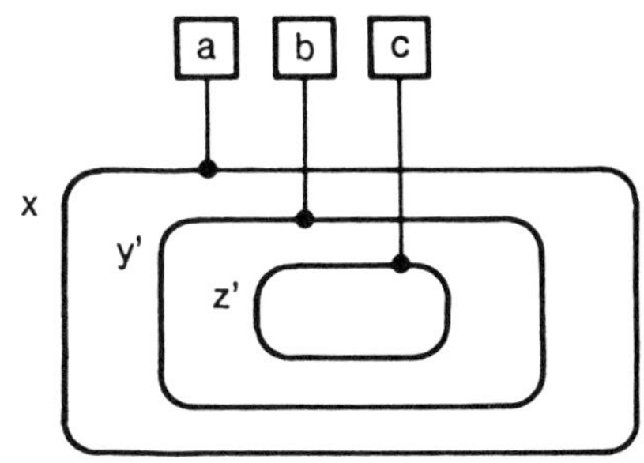

(10) *z*' has locked the object for writing, and associated state *c* has been created as a result.

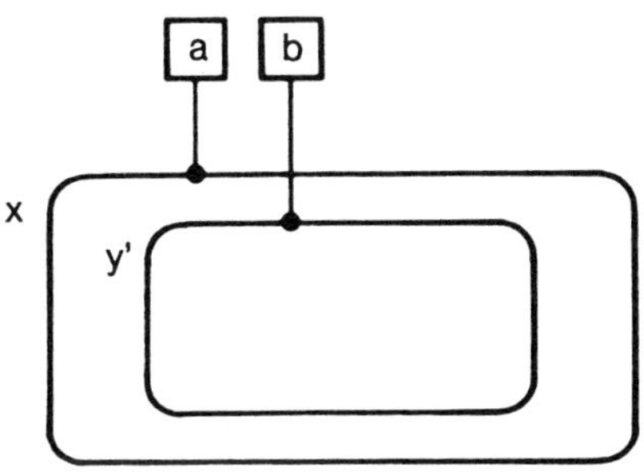

(11) *z*' has committed, but associated state *c* has been discarded by ***y*'** in favor of ***b***.

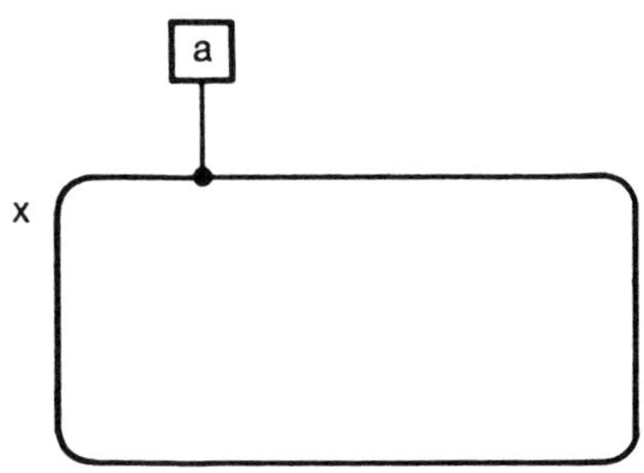

(12) *y*' has committed, and *x* has discarded ***b*** in favor of ***a***.

As in the case of the locking rules, we do not present a proof that the state restoration rules are correct. However, the basic argument is that the associated state for a given object and transaction is always the state to which the object should be restored if the transaction aborts. The associated state is the correct state because it is the first sample taken by the transaction or any of its inferiors. In that sense the associated state is the state that held at the beginning of the transaction. Thus the state restoration algorithm will restore all objects modified by an aborting transaction to the state they had when first accessed by or within the transaction. Hence, other transactions can perceive no effects of the aborting transaction, except perhaps delays resulting from lock waits.

4.4.2 Creating and Deleting Objects.

Object creation and deletion are fairly simple, and though they require special treatment, that treatment is straightforward. Here are the details. Suppose that we have operations called *hard_create* and *hard_delete* that "really" create and delete objects. Then the creation primitive should *hard_create* the requested object, and set the associated state to a special value, *new-object*. The creating transaction holds a *write* lock on the new object, because creation is essentially a writing operation. Should the transaction abort, we will start restoring objects according to the associated states of the transaction. At that time we will see the special *new-object* marker for this object and perform a *hard_delete*, thus restoring the object to its former state, namely, non-existence.

Deletion is somewhat different. When we ask to delete an object, the object is marked *to-be-deleted*, and a *write* lock is set. The commit protocol will do a *hard_delete* of such objects if and when the transaction truly commits. The use of permanent and volatile storage in creating and deleting objects will be described below.

4.4.3 Using Permanent Storage.

The simple approach we take to the use of permanent storage for objects is similar to the approach of the previous chapter. We keep the current object state, and all of the associated states, in volatile memory. Permanent memory contains the old state, that is, the state just after the last successful top-level transaction that modified the object. During two-phase commit (to be described in the next chapter), both the old and current state exist on permanent storage, and later, after completion, the old state is discarded and replaced by the new one. Note that when it comes time to complete a top-level transaction, there is only one associated state for each modified object, and it corresponds to the old state on permanent memory. Hence that associated state could perhaps be discarded, though it might be useful for restoring the volatile version of the object should the transaction end up aborting.

If an object is created by a transaction, the object has no old state, but the associated state for that object would be the special *new-object* marker. The commit algorithms treat that case specially, in order to guarantee that if the transaction aborts then the object will not exist, and if the transaction completes then the object will exist. This special treatment might involve updating some special tables (directories of objects, or whatever). Deletion is handled similarly by the commit algorithm: the object will still exist if the transaction aborts, and is made non-existent if the transaction completes.

A property of our scheme for use of permanent memory is that if a crash occurs before the top-level transaction is prepared, then we have no choice but to revert to the old state on permanent storage. This requires that we abort all transactions holding associated states for the object, and hence all inferiors of such transactions. However, if we wrote more information to permanent storage earlier (i.e., before starting to commit and complete the top-level transaction), then we might be able to avoid aborting so many transactions because of crashes. Using the example of the previous section, if when y committed we saved the current state of the object in permanent memory, being careful not to disturb the old copy there, then we have enough information to recover from a crash more gracefully, and continue from the point just after y committed.

We call such writing of information to permanent memory at subtransaction commit time *early writing*. Early writing is a very restricted kind of *checkpointing*: checkpointing is the saving of intermediate state to permanent memory for the purpose of surviving crashes. That is, a checkpoint is a consistent snapshot of the state of a transaction, including its private and temporary data as well as the states of the objects the transaction has locked.

The idea is that if a failure occurs we fetch the latest snapshot and continue processing from that point, instead of running the transaction from the beginning.

It is conceivable that early writing could simplify the two-phase commit protocol of the next chapter, or reduce its delay. However, if more than one inferior of a top-level transaction updates the same object, then early writing will result in more updates of permanent memory than writing only at prepare time. So it is not clear whether early writing offers an advantage in this regard.

If all we had to worry about was the states of objects, then early writing, and possibly even checkpointing, could be designed without too much difficulty. However, in the general case we must be able to save *all* of *x*'s intermediate data, including its control point, local variables, etc., to be able to continue properly. Checkpointing is further complicated by the fact that the snapshots taken on different nodes must be consistent with each other: together they must represent a consistent intermediate state of the transaction being checkpointed. The feasibility of checkpointing depends strongly on the details of transaction execution - details that are beyond the scope of this work. Therefore, we will not discuss checkpointing further here, though some comments are offered in Chapter 8.

Might we be able to implement early writing alone instead of general checkpointing? Would early writing be useful by itself? To see the answer to the second question, consider two transactions *x* and *y* where *x* is the parent of *y*. Suppose that we perform an early write of *y*'s results when *y* commits. If *x* and *y* are running on separate nodes, and *y*'s node crashes, then the early writing has helped, because we can restore the state of *y*, and *x*'s state is still unaffected because it is on a different node. If, on the other hand, *x* and *y* run on the same node, then early writing of *y* does not help because a crash will abort *x*, forcing *y* to be undone as well. In this case we need to be able to checkpoint *x* (to save its intermediate state) as well as do an early write of *y*'s results.

Even though early writing can help reduce the susceptibility of transactions to failures, it is not really enough: in the example just given, *x* must still always be aborted if it is not checkpointed and its node crashes. It is hard to say whether the improvements in reliability and delay afforded by early writing is marginal or actually very useful, and how much more useful checkpointing would be in comparison. However, since checkpointing is required to really solve the reliability problem, we will not discuss early writing further. A secondary reason for this decision is that omitting early writing will simplify the presentation and arguments of later chapters. If early writing is deemed desirable, it should not be overly difficult to extend the material presented later, though it would introduce additional complexity. So, we will stick with the simplest method of using permanent memory even though it may not be adequate for transactions that run a long time or access a large number of nodes, that is to say, transactions with higher than usual exposure to failure.

Let us briefly comment on another method of achieving resiliency in the face of crashes: logging. Logging does not improve the situation. It has different performance characteristics, but, like the state saving and early writing methods, it lacks the ability to recover a transaction in process. Checkpoints are still required for that, unless something like a hardware recovery cache [LGH80, LS84] is available. Such a cache essentially logs every memory write, which is rather different from the high level logging done in software. However, see also the previously mentioned discussion of checkpointing in Chapter 8.

4.5 New Operations.

In the previous chapter we sketched a possible set of operations on objects and transactions. For the extension to nested transactions we would add some new operations to those already presented:

create_subtransaction (t: *tid*) **returns** (*tid*) **signals** (too_late)

> Creates a new child of *t*. The exception *too_late* is signalled if *t* is no longer running.

get_parent (t: *tid*) **returns** (tid) **signals** (top_level)

> Returns the id of the parent of *t* if and only if *t* is not top-level, and signals *top_level* if *t* is top-level.

is_committed (t: *tid*) **returns (bool) signals** (forgotten)
is_aborted (t: *tid*) **returns (bool) signals** (forgotten)

> These tell whether the indicated transaction has committed (aborted). In some cases memory of the transaction may no longer exist (e.g., after completion or abortion of a top-level transaction); then *forgotten* is signalled. However, a parent should always be able to inquire about a child.

Of course, the semantics of most of the other operations should be changed in the obvious way: the new locking and state restoration rules are followed, commit and abort of subtransactions works as described in this chapter, and so on.

4.6 A Possible Data Structure.

For concreteness we now outline a data structure that could be used for maintaining the locking and state restoration information within a node. We will describe the volatile memory data structures; the organization of permanent memory tables would be somewhat different, but conceptually not as complicated because only top-level transaction information is ever written to permanent memory.[1]

First, to save memory space in the running system, we represent only those locks that are actually in use. When an object is locked, we construct a *lock record* and insert it into two tables. These tables are the *lock table* and the *transaction table*. The lock table maps *object id's* to *lock records*, and the transaction table maps *transaction id's* to *transaction records*, which include a chained list of lock records. The tables would most likely be implemented as hash tables.

Each lock record indicates the mode (*read* or *write*) of lock it represents, and identifies the object locked (by giving the object id) and the transaction possessing the lock. There should be a field for an associated state (probably a pointer to some data whose format we will not discuss), and a slot for the chain linking together all objects locked by the same transaction. The lock records could be doubly-linked for easy deletion from the chain, or might be singly linked, which saves space, but requires searching the chain on deletion. It should be fairly obvious how the locking and associated state algorithms would manipulate the data structure we have described.

---

1. The addition of checkpointing, early writing, or related techniques, would change this, of course.

Here are diagrams showing the most relevant fields of lock and transaction records:

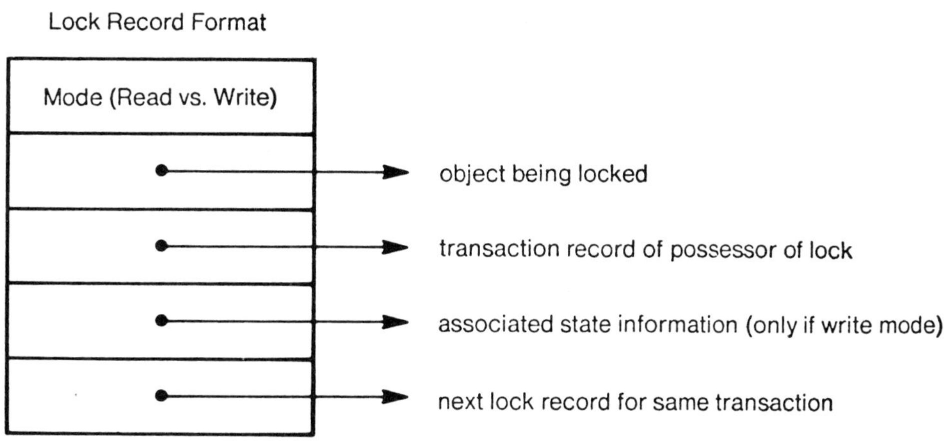

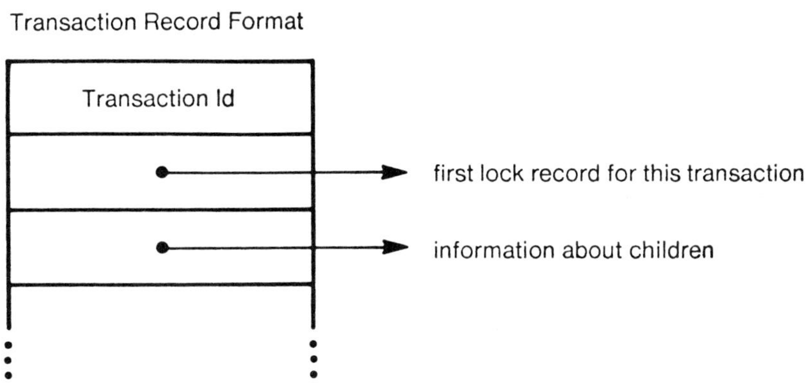

Naturally many other arrangements might be quite reasonable; we are merely being illustrative.

4.7 Summary.

We will present the nested transaction distributed commit protocol in the next chapter; we call it the *transaction management protocol.* Now we will summarize the advantages of nested transactions over single-level systems.

At the beginning of this chapter we mentioned three problems that nested transactions help solve, namely: composing arbitrary transaction routines into larger transaction routines; safely permitting concurrency within transactions; and more graceful response to failures. Subtransactions help with each of these problems as follows:

- Subtransactions permit simple and safe composition of transaction routines that may execute concurrently. So subtransactions enhance modularity.
- Subtransactions are explicitly designed to solve the problems that arise when concurrency is allowed within transactions. The locking and state restoration rules insure this. For a program with concurrency to work correctly, each concurrent thread of computation should be performed with respect to a distinct subtransaction. This simple rule goes a long way towards insuring correctness of concurrent programs in the nested transaction system. The transaction manager presented in the next chapter will assume that this rule is followed. If the rules are broken, consistency might be violated.
- Subtransactions can help protect parts of a transaction from failure in other parts, because the success or failure of each subtransaction is independent of the success of its siblings. Depending on the application's consistency constraints, a parent might *retry* a failed child (e.g., resubmit a request aborted by deadlock), attempt an *alternative* means to the same end (e.g., find another copy of some replicated data), or *ignore* the failure (e.g., update of one copy failed, but enough copies of a replicated item were successfully updated). The failure containment property of subtransactions suggests that most, perhaps all, remote actions should be performed as subtransactions. We will say more about this use of subtransactions in the next chapter.
- Checkpointing may be required for best immunity to failure, but checkpointing schemes are beyond the scope of this work. Further discussion may be found in Chapter 8. However, many applications might not encounter much difficulty with occasional failures; for example, on some systems almost all transactions are quite short (a few seconds to minutes), and unless some system components are unusually unreliable, performance may be quite satisfactory without a

checkpointing feature. Also, it might be easier to improve the reliability of the system by spending more money on hardware (better devices or more redundancy) than it would be to enhance the software. For example, a special highly reliable node could be used for running long transactions (this might require early writing elsewhere).

5. A Transaction Manager Design.

In this chapter we will present the transaction management algorithm for our nested transaction system. The goal is to arrive at an overall organization and detailed protocol that insures that each node commits and aborts exactly the correct transactions. Not quite all of the protocol is presented here: we defer discussion of the means for resolving lock conflicts and potential deadlocks to the next chapter. For now we assume that conflicts and deadlocks do not occur.

5.1 Transaction Management Organization.

Our model of transaction management is that each node runs a *transaction manager*, and all the transaction managers follow the same algorithm. The transaction managers (TM's for short) can be thought of as separate, concurrently running processes, though they need not be implemented that way. The design is distributed, asynchronous, and symmetric. The transaction manager of a node handles transaction-related processing requests, or is at least informed of the relevant details, such as when transactions are created, when they are to be committed or aborted, and so on. To guarantee global consistency, the transaction managers communicate privately among themselves according to the protocols we will develop in this chapter. User communication is entirely independent and uncontrolled. The incorporation of user communication into our transaction management protocols is left as an open problem. Figure 3 presents a diagram of the conceptual relationship between user and transaction manager code in two nodes.

In the previous chapter it was seen that each concurrent thread of computation should be done with respect to a different subtransaction, or else the locking and state restoration algorithms might not work. Actually, it is only concurrency within a single node that can interfere with those algorithms. This is because each object exists entirely at one node; hence concurrent activity under the same transaction id at different nodes will not disturb object states. Since object states determine consistency, if object states are handled

Figure 3. Transaction Manager Relationships.

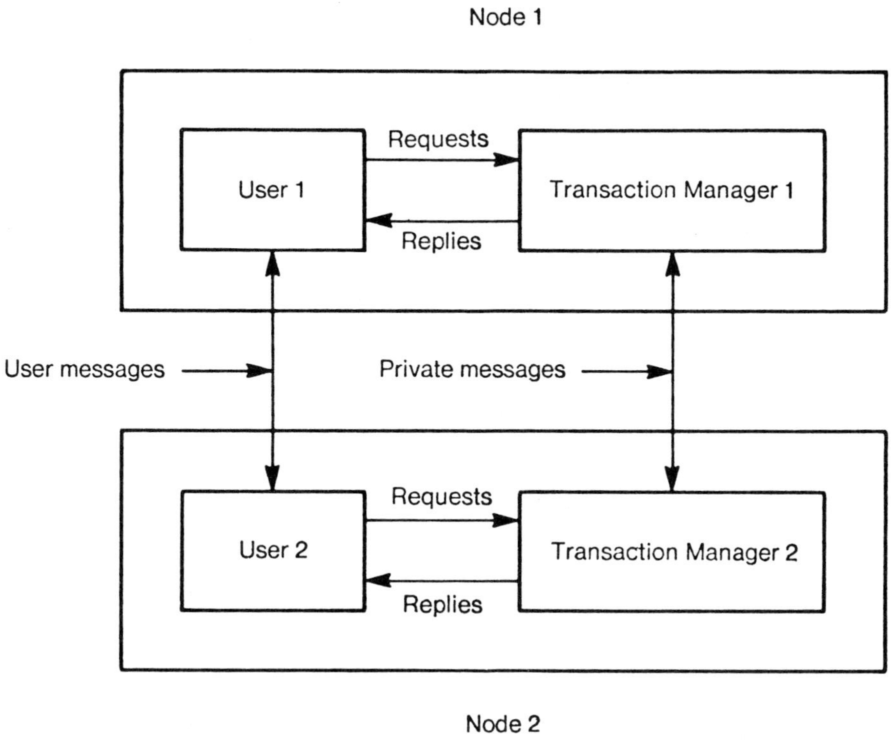

---

correctly locally, then local consistency is achieved.[1] So the designs of the previous chapter do not *force* us to run each transaction at a single node. However, we find it simpler not to distribute individual transactions. Instead of distributing a transaction over several nodes when a distributed computation is requested, each node's part of the computation is performed as a separate subtransaction. Thus each transaction (and subtransaction) is local, and remote actions are always done under subtransactions. Although a transaction may directly manipulate objects only at its home node, it can deal with objects at foreign nodes by creating subtransactions to do the work on its behalf. Note that keeping individual

1. This is not to say that *global* consistency is insured - a large part of the transaction manager algorithms are devoted to turning local consistency into global consistency.

transactions local is a design and implementation decision, and is not required or implied by the nested transaction model of computation.

The advantage in not distributing individual transactions is that the bookkeeping for each transaction is localized to the node on which it is run (called the transaction's *home*). This localization makes transaction management simpler because the status of a transaction is readily determined at the transaction's home without need for communication with or consensus among other nodes. As would be expected, communication among transaction managers is still sometimes necessary. For example, a transaction's inferiors or parent may not reside at the transaction's home, so communication may be required for the transaction managers to coordinate.

We will assume that the home of each transaction is determined when the transaction is created; that is, a transaction's home is part of its identity, and is available to anyone knowing the transaction's *tid*. Being able to derive a transaction's home from its *tid* is convenient for the transaction managers, and is the simplest way of determining transactions' homes. When we speak of the *TM* of some transaction, we mean the transaction manager of the transaction's home node.

We will now attempt to provide some background and intuition before proceeding with the development of the transaction management algorithm. Although a transaction actually runs only at one node, it exists at other nodes in a limited sense. For example, suppose we have a transaction x at one node with a child y at another node. If y commits, then its locks and associated states are inherited by x according to the rules presented in the previous chapter. Because those locks and associated states are useful only at y's home (they relate only to objects there), it is reasonable to keep the records at y's home. Thus a transaction may have locks and associated states at many nodes although it runs and directly manipulates objects only at its home. We will say a transaction has *visited* a given node if the node is the home of the transaction or one of the transaction's inferiors. The nodes visited by a transaction are those that may have lock and state restoration information related to that transaction.

For the locking and state restoration algorithms of the previous chapter to work properly, all of a transaction's inferiors must be *resolved* (committed or aborted) before the transaction itself may be resolved. We will say that a transaction is *locally resolved* at a given node if the necessary commit/abort actions (whichever is appropriate) for that transaction have been performed at that node. Note that the locking and state restoration algorithms require only that a transaction's inferiors be locally resolved before the transaction may be locally resolved. That is, a transaction's inferiors need not be resolved *everywhere* for the transaction to commit or abort *here*. The algorithm we will present takes advantage of the fact stated in the previous sentence. For consistency's sake, we must still make sure that a given transaction either commits everywhere or aborts everywhere, eventually.

A slightly more subtle point is that if one of a transaction's ancestors aborts, it does not matter whether the transaction aborts or commits: even if the transaction commits, its effects will be undone by the abortion of its ancestor. Carrying the point a little further, if one of a transaction's ancestors aborts, then the transaction need not be committed everywhere or aborted everywhere. The reason is that the effects of the transaction will be undone in any case, as just argued. On the other hand, if all of a transaction's ancestors do commit, then the transaction must be resolved the same way everywhere, or else consistency might be violated.

To make resolution easier, we require that all of a transaction's children be resolved before the transaction can attempt to commit. A transaction may abort at any time - it need not wait for its children to be resolved first. Sometimes it might be desirable for a transaction to commit even if the outcome of a child is still in doubt. If that child is at a crashed node, we must wait for the node to come back up.[1] Waiting just to make sure a child aborted seems objectionable; we can avoid it through the following trick. Suppose that whenever we wish to run a child at a different node, we instead run a local child that runs the desired remote action as its child. That is, the remote action is our grandchild. The local

---

1. If we can be sure that the node is crashed, it is safe to assume the child is aborted and proceed. This is because the child's effects cannot have been made permanent, so the crashed node will have no memory of the child, much less its effects. However, if we cannot distinguish a crashed node from one that is slow to respond or one that cannot communicate with us just now because of a communications failure, we must wait for a response from the node. We do not assume that crashed nodes can be detected.

child can be rigged to abort itself when desired. Since it is aborting, it need not wait for its foreign child; and since the local child resolves (by aborting), we do not have to wait. The extra level of subtransactions provides extra control.

It is nice that we do not require transactions to resolve their children before aborting. Not only does it permit us to use the trick presented in the previous paragraph, but it also permits crashes to be modelled as spontaneous aborts of transactions - both crashes and aborts can happen at any time, and have similar results (undoing modifications to objects and releasing locks). The similarity of crashes and aborts will be exploited in the transaction management algorithm. However, if checkpointing or other means were used to prevent a crash from aborting all uncommitted work on the node that crashed, crashes and aborts would be different, and the transaction management algorithm would have to be redesigned.

Because a transaction cannot commit until its children are resolved, the transaction's TM (its home node's transaction manager) must know the identity of each child of the transaction. To satisfy this requirement, if a transaction desires to run a subtransaction at a different node, it will create the subtransaction before sending its request to the foreign node. Suppose that local transaction *x*, running on node 1, desires to run a subtransaction on node 2. To do so, *x* gets node 1's transaction manager to create a subtransaction id suitable for use at node 2. Then *x* includes this id in its request directed at node 2. If *x* really wanted to run an initially unknown number of subtransactions at node 2, all resulting from the one request, those subtransaction could be children of the single subtransaction that was created in advance. Hence, the scheme does not appear to be overly inflexible. It may seem strange for node 1 to create transactions whose home is node 2 (without even telling node 2!), but the method does guarantee that all of a transaction's children are known to the transaction's TM, which was the goal.

In sum, we introduce an operation that creates a transaction id at one node for a transaction whose home is another node. However, this operation is used only when the created subtransaction's parent is located at the creating node. We assume that any transaction id created locally for work at a foreign node is actually used. If the id is not used, then our algorithm will believe that the transaction effectively aborted, because it is as if the id were lost. Even if the creating transaction manager tells the foreign transaction manager about the id, we still have no way to know whether the user's request was processed or not, because we have no control or knowledge of user-level communication. Hence we will not bother to tell the foreign transaction manager about the created subtransaction. Because an unused id looks like an aborted transaction, if it is possible that a transaction id might be created but not needed at the foreign site, the foreign site should at least commit the transaction (which is trivial for a transaction that does nothing).

One of many possible formats for (sub)transaction id's supporting these manipulations is illustrated below.

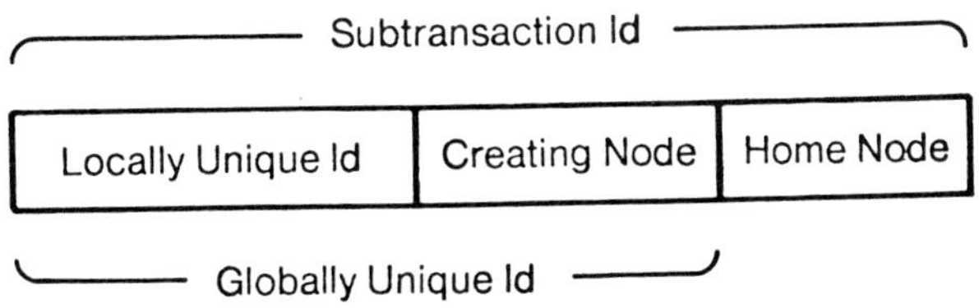

A full (sub)transaction id consists of a sequence of subtransaction id's concatenated together. The first subtransaction id would be the one for the top-level transaction, a subtransaction id for one of its children would be next, and so on down the transaction tree to the subtransaction being identified. Thus a transaction id identifies all the ancestors of its transaction by explicitly enumerating them along the path from the root to the transaction. Hence transaction id's are variable in length. If this is inconvenient for some purposes, transaction id's can be entered in a table and local indexes into that table can be used within a node. Full id's will be used when communicating transaction id's to other nodes. We expect that transaction nesting will not be very deep (because it is analogous to nesting of procedure calls, which is not usually very deep), but it is unreasonable to place small bounds on nesting depth.

Consider again the (top-level) transaction *x* on node 1 that creates an id for *y* to be run on node 2. The transaction id's for *x* and *y* would look like this:

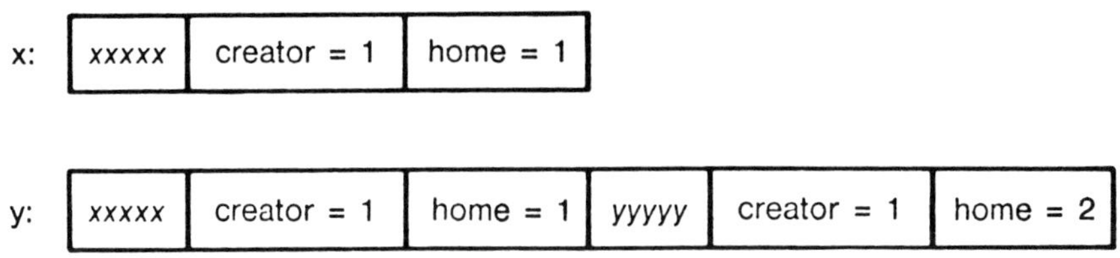

xxxxx and *yyyyy* are numbers unique on node 1

5.2 Normal Case Protocol.

We will describe the transaction management protocol in four stages. This section considers a protocol that works provided there are no failures, no lock conflicts or deadlocks, and no transaction aborts. The following three sections relax these restrictions one at a time: the second scheme handles communications failures, the third additionally handles transaction aborts, and the fourth scheme improves on the third scheme by handling node crashes. Consideration of lock conflicts and deadlock is postponed until the next chapter.

Each of the four algorithms works under the assumptions of its corresponding section. That is, we are not starting with a simple "buggy" scheme and fixing bugs. Further, the addition of new problems or failure modes in later sections does not make the earlier algorithms wrong - the earlier algorithms were not intended to handle the later problems. We believe that presenting the protocol in steps helps to highlight the underlying algorithm and to explain what each part of it is doing (i.e., what problem(s) each part solves).

A transaction's TM is the only transaction manager that can move the transaction through its state transitions towards commitment or abortion. Other TM's that need to know the transaction's state will be informed of state changes via inter-TM messages. Although a transaction's TM is the only manager that can change that transaction's state, state changes may sometimes be forced - it is occasionally required that a transaction be aborted (e.g., to break a deadlock), and crashes, which effectively abort transactions, can occur. However, this does not concern us just yet, because we are assuming for the moment that no transactions abort and that there are no node failures.

Below is a diagram of the possible states of a transaction and the state transitions. We will embellish it with more states later.

Transaction State Diagram

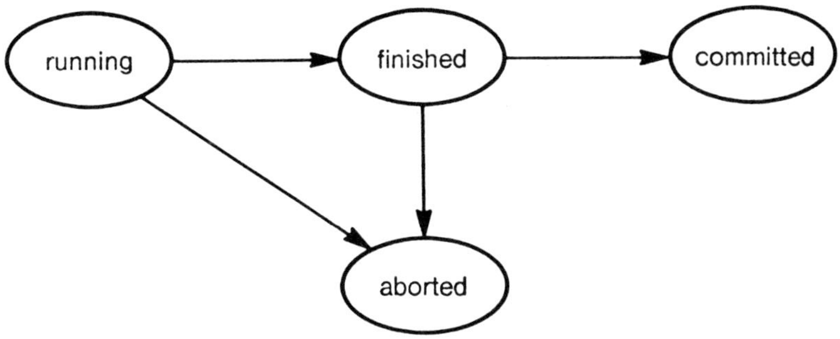

The top row of states in the diagram illustrates the history of a successful transaction. The transaction is initially in the *running* state, which indicates that it exists but is not ready to commit. When the transaction has performed all work it desires to do, it will enter the *finished* state, by telling its TM that it is done. When it is determined that a committing transaction's children have terminated acceptably[1], the TM moves the transaction from *finished* to *committed*. Thus a transaction is explicitly created, and enters the *running* state as soon as some operation is performed with respect to its *tid*[2]. When the transaction has performed all work it desires to perform itself, it so informs its TM, and thus enters the *finished* state. Later, when all the transaction's children have committed, or immediately if they are already committed, the transaction enters the *committed* state.[3]

When a transaction commits[4], a number of TM's may have to be told. In particular the transaction's parent's TM must be informed. But we must also inform all TM's of inferiors of the committed transaction. This is so that the locks and associated state information at those nodes may be updated. The updating is organized as follows. When a new

---

1. That is, all children that the parent requires to commit must have committed. The rest of the children may be either committed or aborted, but may not still be running.
2. In general a transaction need not be known to the transaction manager as soon as its id is created, even if the id is created locally.
3. Under the present assumptions, a two-phase commit protocol is not necessary, because there are no crashes or other failures. Naturally, two-phase commit will be introduced later. At that time we will see that a *committed* transaction's effects are not permanent: the transaction must be *prepared* and then *completed* for its updates to become permanent.
4. Recall that we are not yet admitting transaction aborts, so we do not need to discuss the abort case.

transaction is encountered at a node, the TM insures that there are entries for all ancestors of the new transaction; this may entail creating a number of new entries. These entries are used for local bookkeeping: to keep track of locks, associated states, etc. As previously mentioned, when a transaction commits, the TM's of all the transaction's inferiors are told of the commitment. This permits them to adjust lock and state restoration information. As soon as a transaction has committed and the necessary adjustments to other tables have been performed, the transaction's entry in the TM's data base may be discarded. Any information that is still pertinent has been moved to the committing transaction's parent's entry. When a top-level transaction commits, permanent memory updates are performed, at all sites visited by the transaction. After a top-level transaction is committed, all information concerning it and its inferiors may be discarded.[1]

This first algorithm requires keeping track of the set of nodes visited by each transaction. This is most easily done by associating that set directly with the transaction in the TM's data base. When the transaction commits, the list is used to determine which TM's to tell about the commitment. The list is also sent to the parent's TM, which adds the set of nodes to the parent's set. Hence by the time the parent is ready to commit (when all of its children are resolved), the parent's TM has a complete and correct list of the nodes visited by all the parent's inferiors. The parent's TM should also include all nodes where the parent's children ran (these might not be included in the children's lists).

Here is an example to illustrate the first protocol design. Suppose that each of the transactions in Figure 4 is on a different node; we use their transaction id's to name their TM's. The figure presents both a global state, which is fictitious since it is not necessarily perceived by any node, and the view seen by *y2*'s TM, just to illustrate what such a view is like. The view at each TM varies because it sees only its local transactions, their children, and their ancestors.

This initial algorithm is not at all robust, and is presented only to show the overall organization and intent of the final protocol. The rest of the mechanisms we introduce are

---

1. Actually, it is not until the transaction is *completed* that the information may be discarded; see the later discussion of two-phase commit.

Figure 4. Example of Commitment.

Global State	Visited node sets	View at y2

Snapshot 1: All transactions started, none committed.

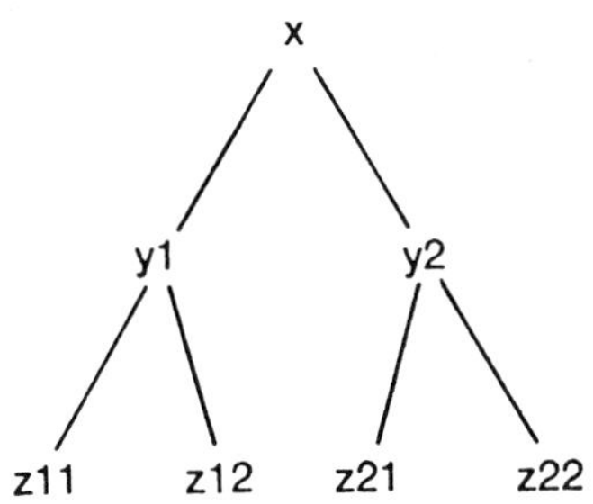

x: { }
y1: { }, y2: { }
z11: { }, z12: { }
z21: { }, z22: { }

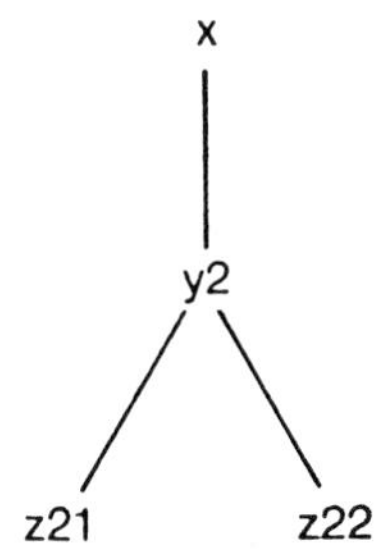

Snapshot 2: z11 and z21 committed, y1 and y2 informed.

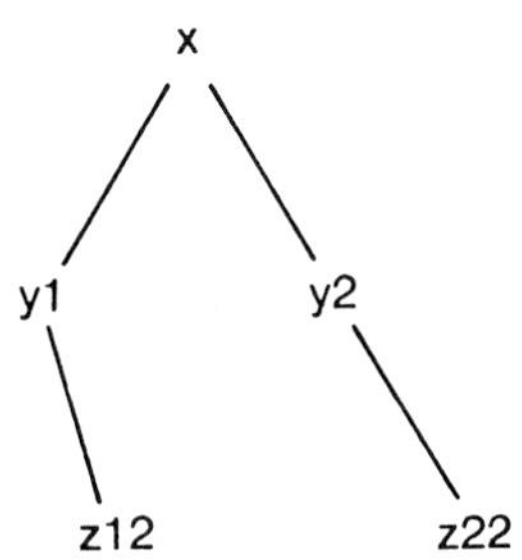

x: { }
y1: { z11 }, y2: { z21 }
z12: { }, z22: { }

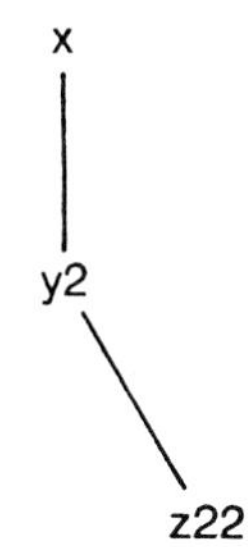

Snapshot 3: z12 and z22 committed, y1 and y2 informed.

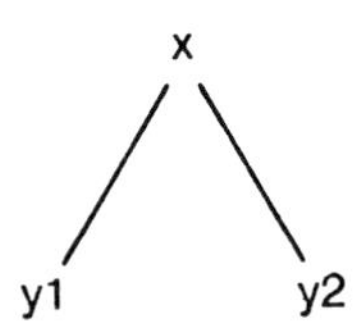

x: { }
y1: { z11, z12 }
y2: { z21, z22 }

Snapshot 4: y1 committed, x informed.

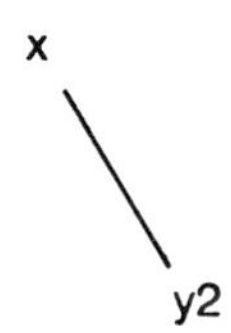

x: { y1, z11, z12 }
y2: { z21, z22 }

Snapshot 5: y2 committed, x informed.

x

x: { y1, z11, z12, y2, z21, z22 }

x

proposed to deal with failures of various kinds. However, the basic approach of passing information up the transaction tree on commitment and broadcasting[1] to all nodes touched by inferiors will be retained throughout. Broadcasting to all visited nodes is a kind of optimization: the simplest, most "natural" algorithms would pass information up and down the transaction tree. But broadcasting can be much faster and use many fewer messages, which is why we use it from the start.

5.3 Handling Communications Failures.

This section presents the second transaction management protocol. This protocol will handle communications failures, but not node crashes or deadlocks, and it does not permit transaction abort. We provide support only for failures associated with transaction manager messages, because we are not specifying user-level communication in detail.

The methods used for dealing with communications failures are simple. Of the possible problems (lost, delayed, and duplicated messages), lost messages are the hardest to handle. Our solution is: if a TM does not hear about a transaction of interest (which transactions are "interesting" and when will be explained later) within some period of time, it *queries* the transaction's TM. Such queries should be repeated until a response is elicited, or is no longer required. With the present set of failure possibilities, only two kinds of querying are needed.

The first kind of querying is called *parent querying*. Suppose a transaction x has children at other nodes. If x is in the *finished* state, then x's TM should query the TM's of unresolved foreign children. Querying should also be performed if the transaction explicitly inquires about the state of foreign children or waits for them to be resolved. Parent querying is necessary for two reasons. One is that the message requesting the child to be run at the foreign node may have been lost - hence, no commit notice would be forthcoming. The other reason is that the child may have run and a notice that it has committed may have

---

1. As mentioned in Chapter 2, we use *broadcasting* to mean the sending of an identical message to a number of different recipients. Our type of broadcast could be implemented using a broadcast medium, if one is available, but separate point-to-point messages would also suffice.

been sent, but the notice may have been lost. Parent querying helps detect these situations. We will explore some details in a moment after discussing the other form of querying.

Parent querying solves the problem of lost commit notices directed from children to parents, but what about lost commit notices from a transaction to its visited nodes? The solution is to have the visited nodes query the transaction's TM. We call this form of querying *participant querying*, because the visited nodes have participated in the transaction. (Later it will be seen that the visited nodes are the participants of the two-phase commit protocol, which also justifies the chosen terminology.) Whenever there are resources held by a foreign transaction (because a local inferior of the transaction committed), and it is important that those resources be freed (e.g., because another transaction is in a lock wait for some of the objects held by the foreign transaction), then participant querying should be done. As with parent queries, participant queries should be repeated periodically until a response is returned or the query is no longer necessary. This retransmission of queries solves the problem of lost queries and responses.

We now have the following kinds of transaction manager messages:

- commit notices
- parent queries
- participant queries
- responses to queries

Responses will indicate the status of the queried transaction, namely *running*, *finished*, or *unknown* (meaning the queried node has no record of the queried transaction). Note that once a transaction has committed, it is then unknown. This leads to a problem. Suppose a child is queried by its parent and the response is *unknown*. What is the state of the child? We cannot tell whether the child has committed or not, because *unknown* is replied in the case where the child has not yet started and also in the case where the child has run and committed. It is easy to remedy this problem: the identities of local committed transactions should be remembered by each TM. With this change, a parent query of a committed child results in the response *committed*, because the foreign node remembers the committed child. It would be unfortunate if the foreign node had to remember committed transactions forever; in this case the identity of a committed transaction need be remembered only until its parent commits, for once the parent commits, no more parent querying of the child will be done.

Duplicate and delayed parent queries and responses to parent queries now pose no problem, because the states of a child form a total order:

$$\textit{unknown} < \textit{running} < \textit{finished} < \textit{committed}$$

Consider all the responses to parent queries of a given transaction. Let *s* be the response that is maximal in the sense of the above ordering. Then we can conclude that the state of the child at its home is $\geq s$. The total ordering of child transaction states allows us to detect the out of order messages that matter in much the same way that sequence numbering would.

Participant queries are less tricky, because we know for sure that the queried transaction must have been running at some time (otherwise it could not have created subtransactions, etc.). Hence a response of *unknown* to a participant query unambiguously implies that the queried transaction has committed. The previously used principle of totally ordered transaction states permits us to handle responses to participant queries that arrive out of order. However, the state ordering for participant queries is:

$$\textit{running} < \textit{finished} < \textit{unknown} \;\; (= \textit{committed})$$

Since query and response messages could be delayed arbitrarily, it is possible that a response would come in even after the queried transaction has been resolved at the querying node. Such responses can just be ignored. The most subtle case involving delayed messages is when a parent query arrives at the child node after the *parent* has committed. The response would be *unknown*, even if the queried child committed. However, this incorrect response will be ignored because the querier is the parent, and the parent has already committed. (It is crucial that the parent commits first at its home and only then at the others node it visited.)

In sum, communications failures are handled by introducing querying. Querying overcomes the problems introduced by lost commit notices and subtransaction requests.

Queries are retransmitted so that it does not matter if they are lost. We found that certain information must be remembered to permit unambiguous answers to parent queries. Namely, the identity of a local committed transaction must be remembered until its parent (locally) commits. We exploited the total ordering of transaction states to solve problems of duplicate and delayed messages and messages arriving out-of-order; it was not necessary to introduce any other form of message sequence numbering.

5.4 Handling Aborts.

The third scheme handles transaction abort as well as communications failures. It will be useful to discuss the semantics of abort in more detail. In particular, in which cases should a parent be aborted because one or more of its children aborted? As argued in the previous chapter, we should permit the user transaction to decide which children are essential and which are not. However, to help protect against oversights in programming, we suggest that the TM abort the parent unless explicitly told to ignore the abort of a child. This feature requires that there be some way for a transaction to tell the TM "it is all right that my child *x* aborted". When the TM is so instructed, it will set a flag associated with its entry for that child. We can represent the situation by adding a new, somewhat fake state to the transaction state diagram. The new state is called *revoked*:

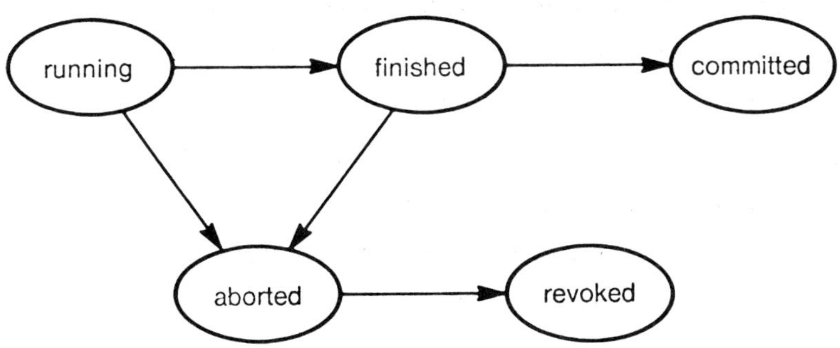

The *revoked* state is fake because it never really exists at the revoked transaction's TM, but only at its parent's. The parent can cause the transaction to be revoked only if it knows the transaction has already been aborted. We emphasize that from the standpoint of the revoked transaction there is *no distinction* between *aborted* and *revoked*. We will say that a transaction is resolved if its state is *committed*, *aborted*, or *revoked*. The commit rule is: a transaction cannot commit unless its children are all resolved and none of their states is *aborted*. That is, each child must be either *committed* or *revoked*. The concept of revoking is not essential, but seems like a good idea in our relatively unstructured system.

When a transaction aborts, all of its inferiors should also be aborted. However, because we do not require an aborting transaction to wait for its children, the inferiors might still be running. Transactions that should be aborted but happen still to be running are called *orphans* (because their parents are "dead" and they are "alive").

There are several adjustments we make to the algorithm so that aborts are handled correctly. First, when a transaction aborts, it is a good idea to inform all its inferiors' TM's of the abort. These abort notices will help free resources at those nodes promptly.[1] But just sending abort notices is not enough, because the notices might be lost. Rather, we would like both parent and participant queries to be able to tell if a transaction aborted. For queries to work, we need to be able to tell unequivocally whether a transaction has committed or aborted, so long as any activities started by that transaction might exist (for participant queries) or until the transaction's parent is resolved (for parent queries). We will return to this point in a moment.

Here is an example that illustrates a second problem. Suppose that a transaction *x* had two children *y* and *z*, and that *y* committed and *z* aborted, and then *x* committed. Further suppose that some node missed the notices that *y* committed and that *z* aborted, but now hears that *x* has committed. This node must query about *y* and *z* to resolve them before committing *x*. However, we suggest a simpler method: each transaction collects the identities of its successful (committed) inferiors. When a transaction commits, its set of successful inferiors are sent out with its commit notices, so that its parent can add them in with its own successful inferiors, and also so that each node visited by the committing transaction can immediately resolve any inferiors of the committing transaction that may be in doubt there. So that responses to queries can return the same information, a TM should

---

1. This assumes that we have some way of aborting running transactions. Some techniques for aborting running transactions are mentioned in Chapter 8.

remember the committed inferiors of each local committed transaction.

The admission of transaction abort requires some adjustments to querying. First, note that the possibility of aborts destroys the total ordering of child transaction states that was used in the previous algorithm. This is because a transaction can be *running*, say, and then it can abort, which would result in responses of *unknown*. The solution to this difficulty is to have two different sorts of parent queries: one is used before the parent knows whether or not the child has started processing, and the other is used if the parent knows the child has definitely started. Further, the responses to parent queries are flagged as to which kind of parent query prompted them. Let us call the first kind of query a *query-new* (because we are querying a new child, not yet known to be established), and the other kind a *query-old*. The matching responses are *response-new* and *response-old*. We now derive the following new ordering:

$$unknown_{new} < running < finished < committed$$

also:

$$finished < unknown_{old}$$

By $unknown_i$ we mean a *response-i* of *unknown*, where *i* is either *new* or *old*. The new *revoked* state does not enter into this ordering because it pertains only to the state of the child at its parent's node, not at the child's own home.

We could have solved our problem by remembering the identity of local aborted transactions, the way we remember local committed transactions. The reason we did not use that technique is to keep the effects of aborts similar to those of crashes - in a crash the identities of the effectively aborted transactions would be forgotten at the crashed node.

The result of the above refinement to parent querying is that we will never think a child aborted when it did not, and we will never think a child committed when it did not. When we admit crashes in the next algorithm, it will be possible for a child to run and either abort or commit, and then for its node to crash, and the overall appearance to the parent could be as if the transaction never even started. However, because the crash wiped everything out, it is as if the transaction never ran, so the distinction does not really matter. Perhaps this gives more insight into what parent querying achieves.

We have removed the potential ambiguity of *unknown* responses to parent queries, but what about participant queries? In the previous scheme (the second algorithm) a response of *unknown* to a participant query always meant the transaction had committed. Now it could mean the transaction aborted. The solution is to remember more information. In particular, each TM will remember (the identities of) all local committed transactions. This permits the TM to look up a queried transaction and reply *committed* instead of *unknown* if the transaction indeed committed.

At this point we have an algorithm that works, but it requires potentially large amounts of information to be remembered. While it appears necessary that the information be kept for a while, perhaps we can find a way for TM's to get rid of it eventually. First, if a TM receives an abort notice for some transaction, it can forget that transaction and all the transaction's committed inferiors, because they aborted. A TM will eventually discover all relevant aborted transactions through querying, and those transactions and their inferiors will be forgotten. However, if a top-level transaction commits, it and its committed inferiors will still be remembered.

Suppose we require some extra steps to be performed when a top-level transaction commits, with the intention of permitting the transaction and its committed inferiors to be forgotten. A first step would be for the TM of the top-level transaction (hereafter called the *top TM*) to retransmit commit notices until it receives acknowledgments from all nodes that ran committed inferiors of the transaction. This would guarantee that all relevant nodes knew the transaction committed.

Perhaps the identities of the inferiors could be forgotten when the commit notice arrived? Unfortunately, no. Suppose that the top TM is in the process of sending the commit notices, that x is a successful inferior of the transaction being committed, and x's node has received the commit notice from the top TM, acknowledged it, and forgotten all inferiors of the committed transaction (including x, of course). If a participant query about x now arrives at x's node, then the response would be *unknown*. Inconsistency would result if this response gets to the querying node before the commit notice that has been sent by the top TM. (The querying node (call it q) initiated the query because x held resources at q. Hence x had committed inferiors at q, and since x is a successful inferior of the top-level transaction, these committed inferiors are successful inferiors of the top-level transaction, too. Therefore q will indeed get a commit notice from the top TM.)

A top-level transaction commit scheme that *does* permit committed transactions to be forgotten is the following: once the top TM has received acknowledgments from all participants as in the scheme just suggested, it sends a *second* round of messages letting each participant node know that it can now forget the transaction and its committed inferiors. To insure that all possible forgetting is done, the top TM should keep sending the *forget* messages to each participant until an acknowledgment (call it a *forgotten* message) is received. Then the top TM can also forget the transaction. The reason two rounds of messages works is that the first round removes the need for querying and resolves the top-level transaction and its inferiors everywhere (except for orphans, which will be discussed in a moment). Once the transaction is committed everywhere it need be, we can safely forget it. The similarity between the two rounds of message passing in the top-level transaction commit protocol and in the two-phase commit protocol is not coincidental, as we will see in the next section.

Orphans do not undermine the scheme just presented. This is because one or more of their ancestors aborted. Hence even if an orphan's TM queries and gets an incorrect response of *unknown*, it does not matter, because the orphan should abort anyway. (Actually, incorrect responses will never arise, but that is harder to argue.)

Our third scheme, just presented, handles transaction aborts and communications failures. The kinds of messages used are commit notices, abort notices, new and old queries, new and old responses, acknowledgments of top-level transaction commit (call these *committed* messages), *forget* messages, and *forgotten* messages. TM's must remember local committed transactions and their committed inferiors. The lists of committed inferiors are included in commit notices, for parents to acquire the information, and for participants to resolve any inferiors that are still in doubt. Transactions may be forgotten if they are known to have aborted, or after a *forget* message for their top-level ancestor has been received. The home of a committed top-level transaction cannot forget the transaction until the transaction is known to be forgotten at all other participant nodes.

Near the beginning of this section we presented a state diagram for transactions. Actually, that diagram applies only to non-top-level transactions; here is a diagram for top-level transactions:

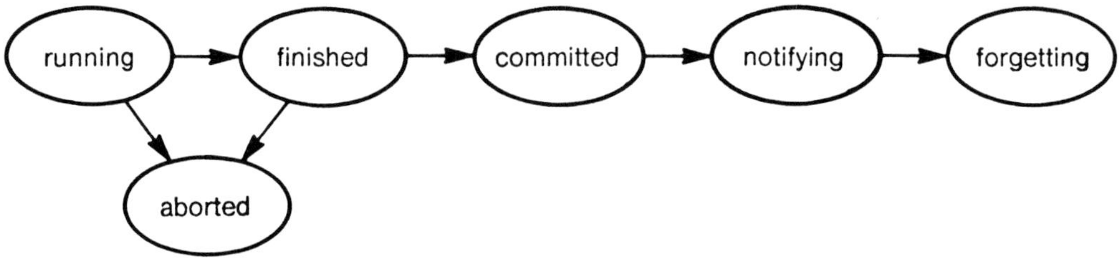

We have added two states, *notifying* and *forgetting*, for the top-level transaction commit protocol. The *revoked* state is omitted because it does not make sense for top-level transactions: they have no parent to revoke them.

5.5 Handling Crashes.

We now present the fourth and final transaction management protocol. It will handle node crashes as well as communications failures and transaction aborts. Crashes introduce only one new situation: a previously committed transaction may be effectively aborted by a crash. This could happen to top-level transactions or to subtransactions. Further, crashes effectively abort running transactions, too. The main adjustment we make to the algorithm is to add two-phase commit semantics to the top-level transaction commit procedure scheme. Since the prepare phase of two-phase commit requires acknowledgments from the participants, it entirely absorbs the notification phase of the third algorithm. Similarly, the complete phase of the two-phase commit protocol absorbs the forgetting phase of that algorithm.

Two important things happen in the prepare phase: each participant checks that crashes have not destroyed transactions thought to have committed; and (if everything is all right) information is written to permanent storage so that later crashes do not affect the participant's ability to commit. Exactly what checks are performed by a participant when it is asked to prepare? As in the third scheme, the participant must resolve any currently unresolved inferiors of the transaction, using the information sent along with the prepare message. That information is a list of all the committed inferiors of the top-level transaction being prepared. Transactions that are on the list and unresolved at the participant should be committed; all other inferiors that are unresolved at the participant should be aborted.

Once unresolved inferiors have been resolved, we can check to see if the top-level transaction may be completed. Of all the transactions on the list of committed inferiors, consider the ones whose home is the participant; call those transactions the *needed* transactions. The needed transactions are the ones that must have survived crashes for the top-level transaction to be able to complete. Consider the participant's list of committed inferiors of the top-level transaction. Of those transactions, only the ones whose home is the participant matter; call these transactions the *surviving* transactions. At this point, it should be clear that every surviving transaction is needed (any unneeded inferiors have been aborted in the process of resolving the inferiors). However, there may be needed transactions that have not survived. In that case a crash must have occurred that caused those transactions to be aborted (in effect), and the top-level transaction cannot be completed. In sum, the transaction may be completed if every needed transaction is a surviving transaction; otherwise the transaction must be aborted.

Actual preparing (writing information to permanent storage) is done as in Chapter 3, and the two-phase commit protocol works in the same way. There are a few minor differences:

- Since *prepare* messages must include the list of committed inferiors of the transaction being prepared, the coordinator needs to be given that list. This involves no effort if the coordinator is implemented by the top-level transaction's TM.
- When a participant receives a *complete* message in the second phase, not only should it perform the necessary permanent memory updates, but it can also delete all information relating to the completed transaction. That is, completion includes the forgetting function of the third algorithm.

With the introduction of two-phase commit, the state diagram of a top-level transaction needs to be amended, as shown below:

Top-Level Transaction State Diagram

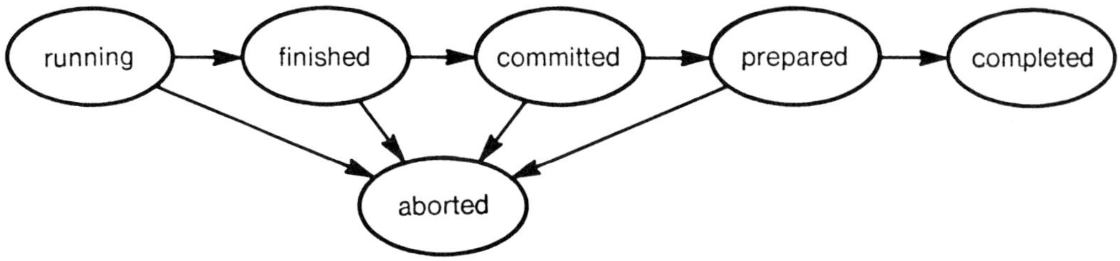

Note that a transaction's effects are not permanent until the transaction is *completed*; that is consistent with the terminology of Chapter 3. Being in the *committed* state only indicates that the transaction believes it was successful - the two-phase commit protocol must be run to insure success (or detect failure).

Crashes do not affect orphan resolution, though they may cause orphans to be created. The only difference is that before we admitted crashes it was possible for us to keep track of all nodes ever involved in a transaction, which would then allow us to go and find all orphans. However, we did not take advantage of that fact, and used a technique (participant querying) that works in the presence of crashes. (That was partly why we chose that technique.)

At this point we have algorithms that guarantee that the correct transactions are eventually committed or aborted everywhere consistently, except for the problems posed by deadlock, which are covered in the next chapter.

5.6 Correctness of the Algorithm.

We now offer an informal correctness argument for the transaction management algorithm just presented.[1] The goal is to establish that if a top-level transaction completes, it and its successful inferiors are committed and completed everywhere eventually; and that unsuccessful (aborted) transactions are aborted everywhere eventually. Further, when a

---

1. A formal proof of some aspects of our nested transaction scheme can be found in [Lynch83].

top-level transaction completes, the "right" inferiors are committed and all others are aborted.

For the moment, ignore crashes that abort transactions after they have committed. Because of the way the identities of successful inferiors are passed from children to parents (i.e., up the transaction tree), an inductive argument would establish that when a transaction enters the *committed* state, it has a correct list of its committed inferiors. This general fact applies to top-level transactions, so when a top-level transaction starts the two-phase commit protocol, its list of committed inferiors is correct. If we consider the effects of possible crashes, then the top-level transaction's list of committed inferiors is an upper bound on the surviving committed inferiors.

Given the correctness of the top-level transaction's list of committed inferiors, it is easy to see that the two-phase commit protocol checks for surviving inferiors correctly, and makes sure that each inferior is either aborted at each of the nodes contacted or committed at each. Hence, a top-level transaction and its inferiors will be aborted or committed correctly at the nodes involved in the two-phase commit protocol.

All nodes where a top-level transaction had successful inferiors will be contacted in the two-phase commit protocol, and the transaction and its inferiors will be resolved correctly as just argued. However, there may be nodes that ran unsuccessful inferiors and which are not included in the two-phase commit. Those node's TM's will eventually discover that the unsuccessful inferiors in question really were unsuccessful, through participant querying.

One part of the argument we have omitted is that each transaction eventually decides to commit or abort. We discuss the issue of transaction termination in the next chapter.

5.7 Summary.

We first explained that the system operates by having a transaction manager running at each node, with the transaction managers communicating privately among themselves to insure correct resolution of transactions at all nodes. Further, each transaction has a home node, and only the home node's TM can change the transaction's state. A transaction's parent's and descendants' TM's will be informed of state changes, but can query the home TM. It is assumed that a transaction's home node can be easily derived from its transaction id. We also explained that a transaction cannot commit until its children have been resolved, but a transaction can abort at any time.

The transaction management algorithm was presented in several stages. First we considered a system in which there are no failures of any kind and no transactions abort or deadlock. That very simple system served to illustrate the overall organization of transaction management, in which information flows from the children's to the parent's TM as the children commit. Then when the parent commits, its TM broadcasts information to all its inferiors' TM's.

Next we showed how to handle communications failures: duplicate, lost, and out-of-order messages. The problems that arose were solved by introducing querying (one TM asking another about the current state of a transaction of interest) and by remembering more information for a period of time (specifically: the identities of local committed children of a transaction, until the transaction itself commits). It was found that the total ordering of transaction states permitted querying to be performed correctly without the addition of message sequence numbering. The same techniques were expanded in later stages of the presentation.

The third scheme permitted transaction aborts in addition to communications failure, but still excluded crashes and deadlocks. Along with aborts came orphans: still running transactions that should be aborted because one of their ancestors aborted. It was seen that the participant querying of the previous scheme is sufficient for finding orphans. We did need to keep around more information about transactions: the identities of all the committed inferiors of a transaction. Further, we needed to add a kind of "watered down" two-phase commit so that information about a transaction could be forgotten once the transaction was done.

In the final scheme we permitted crashes. Deadlocks are not handled by this last scheme; deadlock handling is described in the next chapter. The only new feature required to handle crashes was changing the weak form of two-phase commit into a true two-phase commit algorithm. This involves having participants check in the prepare phase that they can still commit (i.e., that none of the supposedly committed inferiors of the transaction being prepared has been wiped out by crashes), and writing information to permanent memory (as was described in Chapter 3).

In addition to more detailed arguments presented with each scheme, we offered a simple, informal, global correctness argument for the whole scheme at the end.

Here is a summary of the kinds of messages sent between transaction managers in the final scheme:

- Commit notice: This indicates that some transaction has committed. It is sent by the transaction's TM to the parent's TM and also to TM's of all nodes visited by the transaction and its inferiors. The purpose of a commit notice is to bring all TM's up to date concerning the committed transaction. In addition to the identity of the committed transaction, a commit notice contains a list of all the transaction's committed inferiors, to permit resolution of inferiors at TM's that somehow failed to receive the commit or abort notices for those inferiors.
- Abort notice: This indicates that some transaction has aborted. Like commit notices, abort notices are sent by a transaction's TM to its parent's TM and those of all visited nodes. No list of committed inferiors is necessary - when a transaction aborts, all its inferiors necessarily abort.
- Prepare, Prepared, Complete, Completed messages: These message types are used in the two-phase commit protocol. *Prepare* messages carry the same information as commit notices and perform part of the same functions. *Complete* messages need only identify the transaction being completed. If the transaction is aborted in the prepare phase (e.g., because one of the participants cannot prepare), then the usual abort notices are sent to the participants.
- Queries, Responses: Queries are sent from parent TM's to child TM's and from participants to transaction home TM's, to request the latest information concerning the state of a transaction that is in doubt. Parents query children continually to verify that the children actually started running and also to notice if the child's node crashes or the child aborts. Parent queries enable us to recover from lost subtransaction requests and lost commit and abort notices, as well as crashes. There are two kinds of parent queries, *query-old* and *query-new*, which are explained in Section 5.4. Participant queries enable participants to recover from

lost abort and commit notices, and also permit them to discover that they are orphans, if that is the case. Responses indicate a queried transaction's state, or *unknown* if there is no record of the transaction at the queried node. In addition, a response of *committed* will provide the list of committed inferiors of the transaction.

The novelty of our work is that we have shown exactly what information to keep and pass around so that nested transactions can be correctly committed and aborted at each site. It turns out that the list of committed inferiors of a transaction is a sufficient piece of information. While querying involves some subtle points, it is basically a straightforward method for overcoming lost messages. Other techniques might be used to get around communications failures, but querying is simple, and inexpensive if failures are relatively rare.

We have been careful to insure that transaction manager information need not be stored in permanent memory, except for a small amount during the two-phase commit protocol. User transactions do not use permanent memory until two-phase commit either. As pointed out in Chapter 4, a checkpointing mechanism might be desirable, to reduce the vulnerability of transactions to crashes.

We were also careful to make sure that no information need be remembered forever, and we avoided algorithms that are correct only on a statistical basis (e.g., forgetting information after some "suitably long" time has passed). If one makes other decisions on some of these points, one might indeed arrive at a different transaction management algorithm. However, the algorithm we have presented seems to be correct, not only by argument: it has been simulated [Moss81], and parts have been proved [Lynch83].

The next chapter presents the extensions to this chapter's final algorithm to deal with deadlock. The complete algorithm, including deadlock detection, is available in a formal notation similar to a programming language in [Moss81].

6. Guaranteeing Progress.

In this chapter we will show how to make a guarantee that not only does the system as a whole make progress, but also that each transaction request makes progress in the system.[1] It is not possible to make an absolute guarantee, for reasons described below. Naturally, we can make no guarantees at all about improperly programmed transactions.

There are two parts to our guarantee:

- The system will not deadlock.
- The system will not forever abort a transaction request that is properly formed (has no errors in it). That is, if a well-formed request is retried each time it fails, it will be completed eventually.

The second guarantee is the one that cannot be absolutely insured. There are two reasons the second guarantee cannot be met:

- Failures may cause the request to be aborted each time it is attempted.
- The request may be non-terminating.

Note that non-termination may not necessarily be the result of programming errors leading to infinite loops. For example, suppose a particular transaction is to process all files in a given directory. Other transactions might continually create new files so that there is always a queue of work for the transaction in question. The never ending queue is a kind of "livelock" possible in our design.[2]

The main contribution of this chapter is the distributed deadlock detection algorithm for nested transactions. In the next section we first provide some background on deadlock in general, and then present our algorithm in the following steps. First, a naive (but incorrect) algorithm is discussed, to give intuition as to the approach taken. Then we offer an

---

1. Recall that a transaction is an instance of execution of a transaction request. Transaction requests are what are submitted to the system for processing.

2. One might think that since a distributed system such as ours is probably asynchronous, the *arbiter problem* might arise. It has been argued on theoretical grounds and shown by experiment [CW75] that arbiters (binary decision modules) for asynchronous systems cannot be guaranteed to make decisions in bounded time. However, we do not require that progress be made in bounded time, only that it be made eventually. So the arbiter problem is not relevant to our guarantees.

algorithm that works in the absence of failures. After arguing the algorithm's correctness, we point out how to make it robust. Lastly some performance improvements are made to the algorithm. After the deadlock detection algorithm has been presented, we discuss a simple technique for avoiding cyclic restart, starvation, etc. In short, we make about as strong a guarantee as possible that each transaction request will be executed eventually.

6.1 Deadlock.

There are essentially three ways of handling deadlock in a system:

- Prevention: guaranteeing that deadlocks can never arise in the first place.
- Avoidance: detecting *potential* deadlocks in advance and taking action (aborting some transaction(s)) to insure that a deadlock will not actually occur.
- Detection: permitting deadlocks to form, and then finding and breaking them after they have occurred.

6.1.1 Deadlock Prevention.

Deadlock prevention is accomplished by accurately predicting (or bounding) the set of resources a request needs in order to succeed. A request is not started unless all resources it might use are available and guaranteed not to be needed by any requests that have already been started. That is, all resources a transaction needs are reserved in advance.

Not only does deadlock prevention tend to reduce concurrency, possibly by unreasonable amounts, but we must also take into account the cost of analyzing the incoming transactions. Deadlock prevention seems to be impractical except for systems with a fairly rigid, pre-defined structure. A particular advantage of deadlock prevention is that it does not require that any work be undone because of deadlocks, and is the only feasible method in systems with no provision for state restoration. However, the ability to undo work is generally necessary in systems that tolerate failures, so this advantage is not relevant to our design. On the other hand, SDD-1 demonstrates that prevention is not out of the question for many common database applications [BSRG77, BRGP78]. See [CD73] for further discussion of deadlock prevention, including a number of references to other papers.

6.1.2 Deadlock Avoidance.

In avoidance schemes, instead of trying to predict what resources a transaction might require, we simply let the transaction proceed, and take action only when it requests a resource that is not free. The action taken varies with the scheme. It is typical for the requester of the resource to wait for a while, in hope that the resource will be freed. However, if there is a deadlock, then the resource will not become free. Therefore, after the optional wait period expires, either the holder or the requester of the resource will be aborted, on the (overly conservative) assumption that a deadlock has arisen. The simplest schemes simply abort the requester and retry it later. More sophisticated algorithms assign priorities to transactions and abort the lower priority transaction.

Two refined avoidance algorithms that use priorities are the Wound-Wait and Wait-Die algorithms [RSL78]. In Wound-Wait nothing is done unless a transaction starts to wait for a resource held by a transaction of lower priority. If such a wait occurs, the requester *wounds* the holder, causing the holder to abort and free the resource for the higher priority requester. In Wait-Die no action is taken unless a transaction starts to wait for a resource held by a transaction of higher priority, in which case the requester aborts itself (dies). In each of Wound-Wait and Wait-Die the first word indicates the action taken by the requester if its priority is higher than that of the holder, and the second word indicates its action if its priority is lower than the holder's.

Avoidance has the advantages that it is much more flexible than prevention and that it is simple. Avoidance algorithms may abort transactions unnecessarily, though. Say we are using the Wound-Wait algorithm. Then it is entirely possible for a high priority transaction to start to wait for a resource held by a low priority transaction that will eventually finish and get out of the way. But the algorithm will go ahead and abort the low priority transaction anyway.

Deadlock avoidance is more popular than deadlock prevention in data base systems, because it is more applicable than prevention in many cases and also because data base systems tend to incorporate a notion of transaction abort anyway.

6.1.3 Deadlock Detection.

Deadlock detection systems allow transactions to conflict (attempt to acquire the same resources) and wait freely. Rather than trying to steer away from deadlocks, detection methods permit deadlocks to occur and try to find and resolve them after the fact. All deadlock detection methods attempt to find cycles of transactions, each waiting for a resource held by the next. In essence deadlock detection consists only of finding cycles in a directed graph. However, in distributed systems the problem is complicated by the fact that no single node knows all the edges of the graph. It is necessary to communicate some information between the nodes in order to guarantee that all cycles will be found.

The simplest algorithms use centralized detection: all the graph information is passed to some distinguished node, which performs all the graph analysis and sends results back. More sophisticated arrangements use several levels of hierarchy, giving rise to what could be local, then regional, and lastly global deadlock detection. Each level in the hierarchy will find cycles involving larger sets of nodes.

Another class of detection algorithms passes information according to the structure of the graph rather than according to pre-defined responsibilities. The first class is called *hierarchical* detection, with *centralized* detection as a special case. The second class of algorithms are called *edge-chasing* algorithms, because they follow the edges of the graph.

The advantage of detection is that it is less likely to abort transactions needlessly. However, some detection algorithms will find deadlock cycles that no longer exist (these are called *phantom* deadlocks), because of the varying communication delays. Hierarchical algorithms are more subject to this problem than edge-chasing ones. The main disadvantage of detection algorithms is their additional cost and complexity. Detection should abort significantly fewer transactions than avoidance, but the cost of detection must be compared with the cost of the transactions that avoidance would abort and redo. It is also possible that deadlock detection results in lower throughput because transactions holding many resources can queue up for a commonly used resource. This would cause other transactions to back up waiting for the held resources, and so on, clogging the system. It would be interesting if the performance of detection and avoidance were compared in a running system.

6.2 Our Deadlock Detection Algorithm.

We have chosen to present a novel deadlock detection algorithm as the deadlock handling part of our transaction system. The algorithm finds all deadlock cycles, and it does not report many phantom deadlocks (see the later discussion of this subject). One of the previously mentioned deadlock avoidance schemes could have been used to complete our system design, but the detection algorithm is more interesting. Some implementations might be able to get by with deadlock prevention methods, but our design does not require that transactions be that predictable.

As previously mentioned, deadlock detection algorithms work by constructing and analyzing the waits-for graph. A waits-for graph is a directed, bipartite graph in which the nodes represent transactions and resources, and the edges indicate resources held by a transaction, or transactions waiting for a resource. There is a deadlock if and only if there is a cycle in the waits-for graph. Here is an example graph of the minimal deadlock situation: two transactions and two resources:

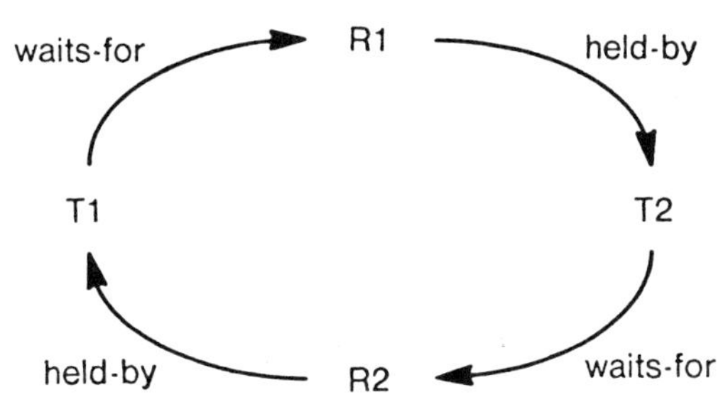

In general, a transaction could be waiting for a complex condition to become true, instead of just for a particular resource to be free. An example of this is a transaction waiting for any one member of a pool of equivalent resources to become available (e.g., a tape drive or communications channel). However, we are dealing with a simpler case, because our resources are the objects of the system, and the only condition a transaction can await is for one particular object to be lockable in a given mode. We will not consider extensions to more complex transaction wait conditions, though such extensions might not be too difficult.[1] Because a transaction can await only a single lock at a time in our system, we will omit the resources from the waits-for graphs, and represent only the transactions.

6.2.1 Overview of Detection Algorithm.

Our algorithm is of the edge-chasing variety. In fact, it never builds very much of the waits-for graph, but only traces individual paths through it. If any path closes on itself, then a deadlock has been found.

There are three steps in the deadlock detection algorithm. The first step is called *initiation*. Detection is initiated only when a transaction starts to wait for a lock held by another transaction in a conflicting mode, and not always even then (exact conditions will be described later). In the second step, called *detection* (or edge-chasing), edges of the waits-for graph are traced, both locally through each node and also between nodes. The transaction managers do this using their knowledge of transaction states, and also by acquiring information about locks held and awaited by transactions. The final step is deadlock *resolution*, and is performed when a deadlock is actually found. In resolution, we pick some transaction in the cycle found, and cause it to be aborted, so that the deadlock is broken.

6.2.2 The Naive Algorithm.

Here are the details of a naive version of the detection algorithm. There are certain ways in which this version does not work, and it is also not at all robust. However we offer this explanation to convey the main concepts. We will point out the difficulties and necessary refinements later.

Initiation occurs whenever a transaction starts to wait for lock. The desired object and the transaction have the same home (because transactions can request locks only on their

---

1. See [BT83a] for an example of a more general algorithm.

home node), so the transaction's TM can readily obtain information about both the transaction and the requested lock. The TM is informed whenever a local transaction starts to wait for a lock, by suitable calls in the lock management code. The TM then finds which transactions hold (or retain) the same lock in modes conflicting with the mode of the waiting requester. That is, the TM makes a list of all the transactions that stand in the way of the waiter. These transactions are exactly the ones for which there is a waits-for graph edge from the waiting transaction. Since we wish to trace out paths in the waits-for graph, the last step of initiation is the sending of *detect* messages to the TM's of the transactions conflicting with the waiter. The contents of *detect* messages will be described in a moment. Initiation is simply the process of responding to the lock wait by building the list of conflicting transactions and sending *detect* messages to their TM's.

Note that initiation may not happen all at once. For example, a transaction may be waiting to acquire a lock in *write* mode, with new transactions acquiring the lock in *read* mode. In this case, as each new reader acquires the lock, a *detect* message should be sent, because the reader stands in the way of the waiting writer.

Detection consists of the processing and forwarding of *detect* messages by the transaction managers. The basic idea is that when a TM receives a *detect* message indicating that some transaction is waiting for (a resource held by) one of the TM's local transactions, the TM checks to see if the local transaction is also waiting. If so, then the TM sends a message to the TM of each transaction conflicting with the local transaction. Each such *detect* message represents a graph path one edge longer than the one for the incoming *detect* message. Thus, paths through the waits-for graph are built an edge at a time.

The *detect* messages contain the identities of the transactions on the path being traced, in order. So the first *detect* message, sent as part of initiation, will have a list of just two transactions in it: the waiting transaction and the particular conflicting transaction whose TM receives the *detect* message. Note that separate *detect* messages are started along each path: a *detect* message indicates a single non-branching path through the waits-for graph.

When a TM receives a *detect* message and finds that its local transaction (the one at the end of the list in the *detect* message) is waiting for any other transactions, the TM should check and see if any of those transactions is on the list in the *detect* message. If so, then a cycle has been discovered and resolution should be applied.

Here is an example of detection in action. Suppose that top-level transactions *x*, *y*, and *z* are in deadlock, and the last to start waiting is *x*. The sequence of detection events after *x* starts to wait is illustrated in this diagram:

Transaction Relationships	Detect Messages Sent (in order)
Node A: x	A → B: [x, y]
Node B: y	B → C: [x, y, z]
Node C: z	C: deadlock detected

x requests lock L1; L1 held by y
y waits for L2; L2 held by z
z waits for L3, L3 held by x

The above situation could have come about if *y* had a previous (now committed) subtransaction at A, *z* had one at B, and *x* had one at C. There are many other ways we could arrive at this deadlock.

6.2.3 The Correct Algorithm.

For this algorithm we assume that there are no failures in the system; a later improvement will make the algorithm robust. Now, in what way is the naive algorithm incorrect? The main flaw is that it does not take nested transaction relationships into account correctly. This happens in two ways. First, suppose a transaction *x* is waiting for a lock held by transaction *y*. The naive algorithm fails because *x* cannot necessarily obtain the lock when *y* commits. This is because the locking rules imply that (in general) *x* will not be able to proceed until some ancestor of *y* commits. The exact ancestor is the oldest ancestor of *y* that is not also an ancestor of *x*. We will call this oldest ancestor the *awaited transaction*, whereas *y* is the *holding transaction*. The other way in which transaction relationships are not taken into account is that when a transaction starts to wait for a lock, all its ancestors are also waiting for the lock in the sense that they cannot commit until the lock is granted (unless some transaction is aborted, but we cannot count on that).

It would not be unusual for both effects to be present at once:

Transaction Structure

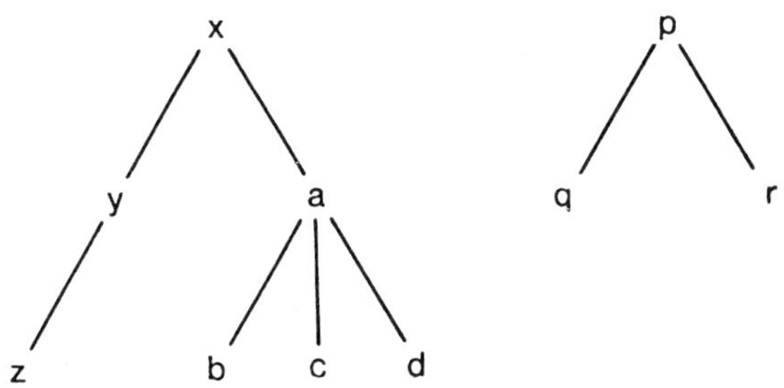

Wait Relationships

z awaits lock L1	b holds lock L1
c awaits lock L2	z holds lock L2
d awaits lock L3	q holds lock L3

Summary of Waits

c → z → b
d → q

Because of the locking rules, *z* cannot acquire lock L1 until both *b* and *a* have committed. In this case *b* is the holder and *a* is the awaited transaction. The most subtle case arises with *c*: it is waiting for lock L2, which is held by *z*. So *c* is waiting for *z* which is waiting for *b*, but *z* is really awaiting *a*, which is an ancestor of *c*. The result is that there is a deadlock between *z* and *a* without *a* holding or waiting for any locks itself. Another situation concerns *d*: it is waiting for a lock held by *q* and is thus awaiting *p*. But none of *p*, *q*, and *r* are waiting for locks, so there is no deadlock.

Based on the above insights concerning the influence of nesting on deadlocks, we propose the following correct algorithm for handling deadlocks:

Initiate detection whenever a transaction starts to wait for a lock; send *detect* messages to the awaited transactions. For example, in the naive algorithm *z*'s TM would have sent a *detect* to *b*'s. Now *z*'s TM will send the *detect* message to *a*'s. However the *contents* of the detect message is the same ([⟨*z*, *b*⟩] in this case). When a transaction acquires a lock in *read* mode, it may be necessary to initiate (i.e., if there are any transactions waiting to acquire the same lock in *write* mode).

When a *detect* message is received for a transaction T (e.g., *a* in the above example), the TM will check and see if T is awaiting a lock. If so, then T and the holder of the lock (call it T') should be added to the list of transactions in the *detect* message, and a new *detect* message containing the longer list should be sent to the TM of the awaited transaction (the appropriate ancestor of T').[1] The contents of *detect* messages now consist of a sequence of pairs where the first member of the pair is waiting for a lock held by the second member. Also the awaited transaction is the oldest ancestor of the second member of the pair that is not an ancestor of the first member of the pair. There is a deadlock if any transactions awaited by T are ancestors of any of the waiters (first members of pairs) listed in the *detect* message.

In addition to sending a new *detect* message to the TM of each awaited transaction, the original *detect* message is forwarded to the TM for each child of T so that we can see if any inferiors of T are awaiting locks. In the example we have been using, *a* would forward the *detect* message it receives from *z* to each of *b*, *c*, and *d*. The message is irrelevant to *b*, which is not awaiting anything. However, *c* is awaiting a lock, and will find that the lock is held by *z* and thus discover a deadlock. Finally *d* will receive a *detect* message containing [$\langle z, b \rangle$] and will send a *detect* message containing [$\langle z, b \rangle$, $\langle d, q \rangle$] to *p*.

Resolution consists of choosing and aborting some transaction in the deadlock cycle. We defer further discussion of resolution until we present the final algorithm.

We claim that the algorithm just presented finds any deadlock that occurs in the system, provided there are no failures (i.e., no crashes or lost messages). To see this, think of a deadlock cycle. Consider the transaction that enters the cycle last and closes the loop, forming the deadlock; call this transaction *x*. When *x* starts to wait, its TM sends a *detect* message to the TM of each transaction that must complete for *x* to be able to proceed. The recipients pass *detect* messages "down the tree", and if any waiting transactions are found, deadlock detection paths are extended by sending more *detect* messages. In short, each transaction for which *x* is directly or indirectly waiting will receive a *detect* message. Since

---

1. Here is how we know where the awaited transaction's TM is. The awaited transaction is an ancestor of T'. We have the *tid* for T' in hand, which, as explained in the previous chapter, includes the *tid* for each ancestor of T'. From the *tid* of any transaction (the awaited transaction in particular) we can derive its home node. That is where we send the *detect* message.

there is a deadlock, *x* is indirectly waiting for itself, so a *detect* message will come back around the cycle and the deadlock will be found. Hence, if there is a deadlock it will be found.

If we assume that waiting transactions are never aborted (even because of deadlock), then it can be shown that the algorithm never claims there is a deadlock cycle when one does not in fact exist. The reason is that for a message to appear to go around a cycle, each transaction must be waiting for the next. Since we just assumed that waiting transactions do not abort for any reason, if a message appears to have gone around a cycle, the cycle must still exist. In this sense no phantom deadlocks are detected by the algorithm. We will discuss phantom deadlocks in more detail later.

The algorithm is clearly sensitive to lost messages - deadlocks will not be detected unless the necessary *detect* messages get through at each step around the cycle. A simple way of overcoming lost messages is for each initiator to retransmit its *detect* message periodically, until the waiting transaction is no longer waiting (aborted, or acquired the desired lock). The repeated receipt of this *detect* message by the awaited transaction's TM induces periodic retransmission there, and so on down the path. We suggest that this form of retransmission be used, without any acknowledgments flowing in the other direction, because it is a simple and relatively cheap way of overcoming communications failure.[1] It also solves some potential problems with improvements we are about to suggest, as we will explain later.

Node failures do not interfere with deadlock detection (except by causing detection of phantom deadlocks), because the only side-effect of a node failure is to cause transactions to be aborted. Such aborts can only break deadlocks, not make them. We have argued that the algorithm presented will in fact find all deadlocks in the system. Further, deadlocks will be found with reasonable dispatch, even in the face of communications and other failures. However the algorithm is more expensive than necessary. In the next section we investigate

---

1. We say "relatively cheap" because every alternative we designed involved the use of permanent storage, which is probably more expensive than periodic retransmission, especially in environments where message transport is reasonably reliable.

some techniques for reducing the cost of deadlock detection.

6.2.4 Refinements to the Detection Algorithm.

There are two ways in which the basic algorithm can end up costing more than necessary. First, each member of a deadlock cycle initiates detection. For a cycle of length n, we may end up sending $O(n^2)$ messages before the deadlock is found and resolved.[1] Similar arguments apply to paths through the waits-for graph that do not close into cycles. Another problem is that if a deadlock is discovered at different places along its cycle, then more than one transaction might be aborted to break the cycle. Assuming that our goal is to minimize the number of transactions aborted because of deadlock, it would be better to insure that a particular member of a cycle will always be chosen.[2]

Both problems (that every member of a cycle initiates deadlock detection, and that more than one transaction might be aborted when a cycle is detected) can be alleviated by suitable use of transaction priorities. Assume that every transaction is assigned a priority, fixed for the transaction's lifetime. For current purposes, the only property required of priorities is that given any set of transactions (and their priorities) we can derive a total ordering of the transactions according to priority, and any transaction manager that computes such an ordering will arrive at the same answer. This implies that the priority of each transaction is distinct. The next section will show that using timestamps as priorities is a good idea.

Now, let us see how priorities help reduce the cost of detection. First, if a deadlock cycle is found, the lowest priority transaction in the cycle will be aborted to break the deadlock. Actually it is not the awaited transaction that is aborted. Rather, we find the oldest descendant of the awaited transaction that holds or retains the lock in a mode conflicting with the waiter, and abort that transaction. Thus, the aborted transaction is a

---

1. The messages from n initiators will be forwarded through $O(n)$ nodes (at least).
2. If there are multiple, interlocking deadlock cycles, then (any version of) our algorithm may abort more transactions than absolutely necessary. But such cases are probably rare, and do not invalidate the guarantee of progress explained in the latter part of this chapter.

descendant of the awaited transaction and an ancestor of the original holder. Recalling our earlier example, if *a* had lower priority than *z* then we would abort *b*, the holder of the lock for which *z* is waiting, or we would abort *a*, if *b* has already committed. Aborting the (holding descendant of the) lowest priority transaction entirely solves the problem of different resolutions to the same deadlock.

A second refinement is to initiate deadlock detection only when a higher priority transaction starts to wait for a lower priority one. On the average this technique would cut the number of initiations in half. However, there are subtleties involved in making this improvement. Consider this diagram:

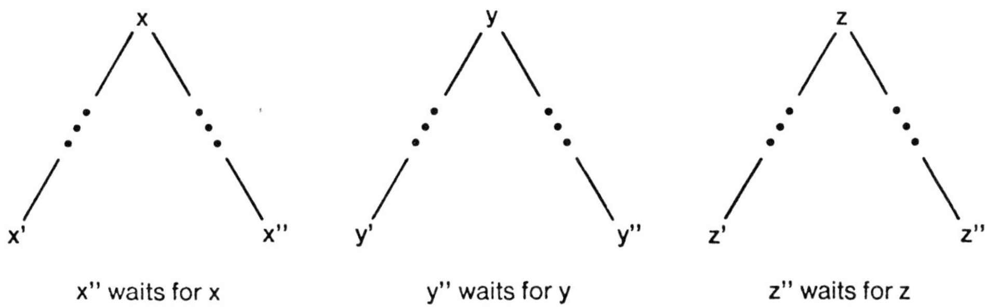

Because the priorities of subtransactions might be somewhat independent of the priorities of their ancestors, we should not compare the priorities of the actual waiter and holder of a lock. Examining the diagram, what really matters is the relative priorities of *x*, *y*, and *z*, since the cycle is really through them, and only intermediately through their inferiors. For example, we would like to initiate the *x''* to *y'* edge if priority (*x*) > priority (*y*), the *y''* to *z'* edge if priority (*y*) > priority (*z*), and the *z''* to *x'* edge if priority (*z*) > priority (*x*).

However, when presented with a single edge of the waits-for graph, as we are when a transaction is just starting to wait for a lock and we wish to decide whether or not to initiate deadlock detection, we cannot know which ancestors of the waiter and holder to compare for a drop in priority. For example, suppose that *x''* just started waiting for *y'*; how do we know that *x* is the ancestor of *x''* that is involved in the cycle? The answer is that we cannot know which ancestor is in a cycle, if any, and must choose conservatively. (Note that if a cycle is found we *do* know the appropriate ancestors and have no trouble deciding which transaction is the lowest priority and will be the victim for deadlock resolution.)

We now impose a requirement on transaction priorities: the priority of any transaction must be less than the priority of each of its ancestors. This is intuitively reasonable because an ancestor probably represents more work, is older, etc.

Given that a transaction's priority is always greater than its inferiors' priorities, we see that it works to compare the priority of the top-level ancestor of the waiter with the priority of the holder when deciding whether or not to initiate detection. This is because the top-level ancestor's priority is the highest possible of any ancestors of the waiter and is thus conservative since we are looking for a drop in priority. However this comparison is slightly over-conservative. We can improve upon it by comparing with the awaited transaction's priority instead of the holder's priority, since it is the awaited transaction that will be on the deadlock cycle. In the example above, we would compare against the priority of *y* instead of the priority of *y'*.

Another adjustment is applicable when the waiting and awaited transactions are inferiors of the same top-level transaction. Instead of using the top-level ancestor of the waiter in the comparison we should use the oldest ancestor of the waiter that is not also an ancestor of the awaited transaction. The general rule is: if *x* is the waiter and *y* is the holder, we compare the priority of the oldest ancestor of *x* that is not an ancestor of *y* against the priority of the oldest ancestor of *y* that is not an ancestor of *x*. Here is an example to illustrate the rule:

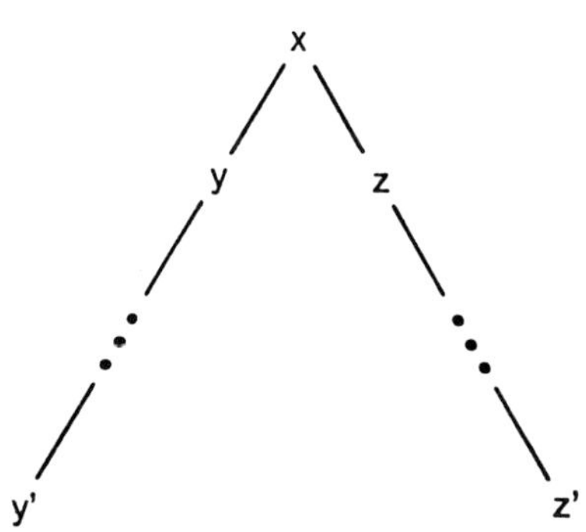

y' is waiting for L
z' holds L
y = oldest ancestor of y' not superior to z'
z = oldest ancestor of z' not superior to y'
initiate if priority (y) > priority (z)

The comparison we propose works because if there is a cycle involving *y'* and *z'* then *z* is a member of the cycle, and *y* is either a member or an ancestor of a member. Suppose that there is indeed a deadlock, and let y'' be the descendant of y that is on the cycle. Then if there is drop in priority from y'' to z (that is, priority (y'') > priority (z)) then y to z also exhibits a drop, because priority (y) $\geq$ priority (y'').[1] The other crucial fact is that every cycle exhibits a drop in priority somewhere. This is seen by realizing that the priorities of the members of the cycle can be totally ordered, so there is a minimal member. The edge to the minimal member from its predecessor necessarily has a drop in priority. Therefore, if there is a cycle, detection will be initiated by at least one edge of the cycle. Thus the refined algorithm will work.

What is the performance improvement? It is easy to see that initiation will occur at about half the members of a cycle (or even of non-cycles), so we have reduced the work performed to about half of the original algorithm. Another technique that will further reduce the number of *detect* messages sent is to ignore certain *detect* messages. Of all the possible paths around a cycle, each beginning at a different edge, we need only one to detect a deadlock. Suppose that we agree to use only the path starting just before the transaction of lowest priority in the cycle. That is, the edge where the awaited transaction has the lowest priority of all the awaited transactions in the cycle. This edge will always be initiated, as argued above. Further, it is the only particular place in a general cycle that is guaranteed to initiate; hence it is a natural choice.

The suggestion is that if in tracing a path we come to a transaction with a priority lower than the awaited transaction at the start of the path, then we can stop tracing the path. It is safe to do this because the edge last encountered must also be a drop and will also initiate. If there is a cycle, the *detect* messages will come up around "behind us". The point is that if we discover that we initiated at a non-minimal point in the cycle then we stop tracing the path in question, and let the path starting at the minimal point do the job. Here is an illustration of this second refinement to our deadlock detection algorithm:

---

1. If y and y'' are different, priority (y) > priority (y''); but if y and y'' are the same then of course priority (y) = priority (y'').

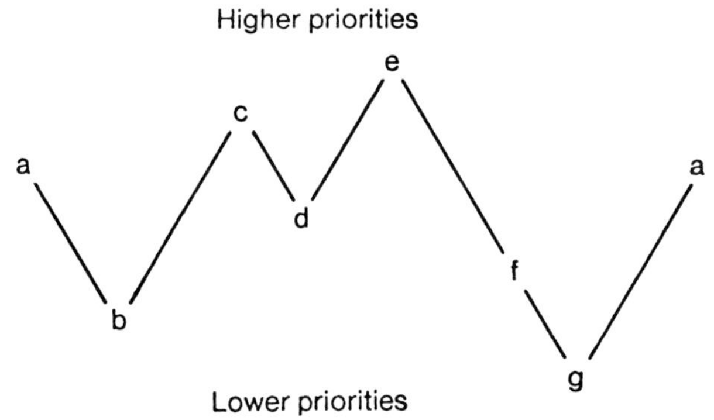

Initiation points are: a, c, e, f
Preferred initiation point is: f
(because g is minimal)

Of the four initiation points, the preferred one is at *f*, and all the other paths will be given up as they reach *f*.

It is possible for more than one path to detect the same deadlock, if all but one of the paths start outside the cycle and enter the cycle at the minimal point. Note that any resulting multiple detections of the same deadlock are harmless: they do not break the algorithm, they only cost more.

The technique just presented cuts down by an average factor of as much as one half the number of messages sent once detection is initiated, because all paths starting on the cycle (except one) will be given up, and the abandoned ones are stopped after going an average of halfway around the cycle. So the techniques put together reduce the number of messages by a factor of two to four, on the average, for large cycles.[1]

The second refinement (discarding certain *detect* messages) may not be very important in practice. For example, an unpublished study of deadlocks in System R [Gray80b] seems to indicate that virtually every deadlock cycle is of length two: they found no deadlocks of length three or more in their study. If that holds up for applications running in our system,

1. This reduction by a factor of four comes from a very simple analysis. We conjecture that the techniques improve average behavior from $O(n^2)$ to $O(n)$, but have not yet discovered a proof.

then there will be only one initiation point for each cycle, and the minimum number of *detect* messages will be sent even without our last performance improvement. Note though that the first improvement (initiating only where there is a drop in priority on a path) still cuts the number of messages in half, and seems to be worthwhile. We cannot give any explicit count of the number of messages involved because it varies with the relative depth of nesting of transactions in the transaction hierarchy. However, if a deadlock is directly between two top-level transactions, it will be discovered and resolved at the cost of sending one message (assuming of course that the message is not lost).

An interesting fact is that the refinements to the original algorithm do not necessarily work if retransmission of *detect* messages is not performed. To see this, consider the previous diagram again. Suppose that *f* starts to wait for *g* before the cycle has entirely formed. Then the minimal initiation will not find a cycle, quite correctly, because the cycle does not yet exist. When the cycle is closed, it will not be detected because all other initiations will stop traversing the cycle when *f* is reached. However, retransmission solves this potential problem: eventually the *f* to *g* initiation will be retried after the cycle is formed, and will thus detect the cycle correctly. So retransmission solves at least two problems at once. Because retransmission is so simple, we advocate using it to solve these problems instead of trying to find separate solutions.[1] Naturally we suggest that the retransmission interval be adjusted to make the correct trade-off between cost of retransmission and delay in finding deadlocks.

Our algorithm does not find many so-called "phantom" deadlock cycles. The reason is that each *detect* message that extends the path is sent only because a transaction is actually waiting. Of course, if a waiting transaction aborts for some other reason (typically a crash), then we may find a phantom cycle. Also, if there are interlocking deadlock cycles, or a new cycle forms with some members that were involved in a previous cycle, needless aborting ensue. All these cases seem rare enough not to worry about. Because of the delays inherent in distributed systems, and because we admit failures, our algorithm probably

---

1. The solutions that occurred to us all involved acknowledgments and permanent storage updates, and so are probably more expensive anyway.

comes about as close as possible to eliminating the detection of phantom deadlocks.

Comparing our detection algorithm with deadlock avoidance algorithms, we find that avoidance algorithms would generally abort a transaction at the points where we initiate detection. Actual performance comparisons would have to weigh lost work (transactions unnecessarily aborted by avoidance schemes) against the *detect* messages and slightly higher complexity of detection. There may also be more subtle effects, such as the previously described backing up of transactions waiting for commonly used resources. We are not prepared to compare avoidance and detection in more detail. However, two things can be said regarding avoidance. First, in avoidance schemes that compare transaction priorities, those priorities should be determined as for for our deadlock detection algorithm: from the priorities of the appropriate ancestors of the conflicting transactions. Second, because of its simplicity and low delay, avoidance might be preferable to detection, especially when transactions are short.

As a side point, we note that the detection algorithm can help make the normal transaction management algorithm work a little better. For example, detection might find that an awaited transaction had in fact been aborted or committed, but some nodes had not yet discovered that fact. Thus an incoming *detect* message might trigger a transaction manager to retransmit commit or abort notices.

6.2.5 Summary of Deadlock Handling.

Instead of deadlock prevention or avoidance, we have presented a novel deadlock detection algorithm. This algorithm works by following edges of the transaction/resource waits-for graph in real time, trying to find cycles. Transactions are assumed to have permanently assigned priorities, and several techniques were suggested for using these priorities to improve performance of the deadlock detection algorithm:

- Start tracing graph edges only when a higher priority transaction waits for a lower priority one.
- Stop tracing a given path if a transaction of priority lower than the one triggering tracing of the path is encountered.

- When a cycle is found, abort (the appropriate descendant of) the lowest priority member of the cycle to break the deadlock.

Initial *detect* messages are retransmitted, to avoid the possibility of cycles' being overlooked, and to make the algorithm robust in the face of failures.

We did not say much about deadlock resolution, except to describe which transaction should be aborted to break a deadlock. Since the transaction to be aborted may still be running, aborting it presents problems similar to those posed by orphans in the previous chapter; see Chapter 8 for discussion of methods for aborting running transactions.

Obermarck [Obermarck80] designed an algorithm based on many of the same ideas. However, our algorithm was arrived at independently; it works for our nested transaction system while Obermarck's algorithm deals with only single level transaction systems; and we offer a novel performance enhancement (stopping propagation of detect messages at low points in the cycle), in addition to the one proposed by Lindsay and included in Obermarck's paper. Another difference is that our algorithm works in an entirely asynchronous fashion, whereas Obermarck's proceeds in more or less synchronized stages. The differences between the algorithms seem minor, yet they might influence the likelihood of finding phantom deadlock cycles. The matter requires further investigation.

6.3 Eventual Execution.

In this section we will explain how to insure that each transaction request will eventually succeed, provided that it is well-formed (will not encounter run-time errors, is not mis-programmed, etc.), and that it is not always aborted by node or communications failures. The technique is based upon the transaction priority concept introduced in the previous section. Here is our idea in its simplest form.

Suppose that we assign transaction priorities based on when transactions are created, so that older transactions have higher priority. This is logical because older transactions have been running longer and are probably more expensive to abort (in the sense of lost work). Hence, older transactions should have higher priority to reduce the chance of aborting them because of deadlocks. Further suppose that it is actually transaction *requests*[1] that are assigned priorities, and that each attempted execution of a request is performed with the same priority (though under different transaction id's). Similarly, retries of failed subtransactions should be performed with the same priority as the failed subtransaction.

Given all the transactions in the system, some one of them will have the highest priority, and thus will never be aborted because of deadlock. Because all deadlocks are eventually resolved (using the algorithms of the previous section), the highest priority transaction is guaranteed to progress and commit, unless failures cause it to be aborted, or it is malformed. Even if it is aborted, when it is retried, it will still be the highest priority transaction, and no other transaction can stand in its way. Thus, unless failures abort every attempt to execute the request, the request will eventually succeed. Then the second highest priority transaction will have the highest priority, and no one will be able to stand in *its* way, etc. This is the sense in which we can guarantee progress of each transaction in the system.

Here are some points crucial to the success of this idea. First, we must make sure that only a fixed number of active requests (either now or in the future) can have priority higher than any given request. If higher priority requests could keep coming along, then a request could be starved. This is why we suggest assigning priorities based on time. For our purposes, clocks at different nodes need not be absolutely synchronized; approximate synchronization will do (see [Lamport78] for a specific algorithm for approximate clock synchronization). Second, when a request is retried, it must be retried with its original priority: lower priorities could lead to its starvation, and higher priorities could permit it to starve other requests. It should be noted that a request's *effective* priority increases with time, since requests with higher priorities leave the system.

It is not necessary that priorities be assigned absolutely with respect to time. An initial increment can be added to a transaction request's nominal priority when the request is

---

1. Recall that a transaction is an instance of execution of a transaction request: users submit transaction requests, and an automatic retry feature (if there is one) might attempt the request several times, each attempt being a separate transaction.

submitted, so as to give it a higher or lower priority. However, such increments must be bounded, or the system could be continually flooded with high priority transactions that would starve normal priority transactions, even ones that had been in the system for very long times. Further, we must be careful to insure that such priority adjustments never make the priority of a transaction as big as that of its parent. To guarantee that priorities are unique, one can simply use the *tid*'s (which are guaranteed to be unique) to break ties. It is all right to use the *tid* of the first attempt of a request as the request's priority. That method is simple, cheap, and sure.

The use of global priorities enables our system to solve problems often left unsolved in previous systems. In particular, many systems admit *cyclic restart*, a phenomenon in which a set of transactions perpetually abort each other (usually because of deadlocks). Our system avoids cyclic restart by aborting only one member of a deadlock cycle, the lowest priority transaction. Even if a system solves cyclic restart, and thus guarantees that the system as a whole makes progress (except if failures are too frequent), it might still permit individual transactions to be starved forever. Most systems solve this problem in a statistical sense: it is very unlikely that any given transaction would be starved forever. While statistical solutions may be practical, we have more confidence in a system such as ours, which cannot exhibit the bad behavior in the first place.

Note, though, that our guarantee of progress is based on the assumption that every transaction will terminate. As discussed at the beginning of this chapter, assuming termination implies assuming that transactions cannot interact in such a way that a transaction's "queue of work" never empties. It is also assumed that transactions do not exhibit the usual kind of infinite loop.

6.4 Summary.

In this chapter we have shown how to guarantee progress of each transaction request in the system, unless failures occur too frequently or unluckily. To achieve this end, we introduced a novel deadlock detection scheme. The use of transaction priorities in the deadlock detection algorithm, and a global strategy for priority assignments complete the scheme. We believe the result is a simple and elegant system, with few layers and *ad hoc* mechanisms. Further, our relatively simple techniques have enabled us to make stronger guarantees than many previous designs.

This chapter completes the presentation of our system design. The next chapter compares our ideas with some specific previous work. We offer some thoughts on extensions and improvements to our work in Chapter 8, and attempt to place the work in broader context.

7. Related Work.

In previous chapters we have sometimes mentioned other specific works in restricted contexts. Now we present a broader recapitulation of work related to ours, in an effort to relate our design with other recent research concerning reliable distributed computing.

Nested transactions are still a fairly new concept, and the novelty of our design lies in that area. We will consider related nested transaction work, including Reed's design [Reed78], at the end of this chapter and will cover other topics first. In order, we will discuss concurrency, reliability, systems addressing both concurrency and reliability, and nested transactions. Note that we have not attempted to be comprehensive in all these areas, because the literature is both large and diverse. However, we have tried to choose representative and significant work to compare with our design.

It should be kept in mind that unless otherwise noted all of the other designs we will discuss are single-level systems. Further, few of the schemes have been implemented, and there are virtually no performance results. Hence, we cannot make quantitative comparisons, only give our qualitative opinion. So we will concentrate on describing the features provided by different designs and the mechanisms used.

In addition to supporting nested transactions, our design also differs from most other work in terms of its context. We were not attempting to design a distributed file system or a distributed data base system in particular. Rather we were aiming for a general purpose system, not directed towards any specific application (within the constraints of the model of distributed systems presented in Chapter 2). Hence we attempted to avoid restrictions. For example, we did not assume predictability of transaction requests, a major difference between our scheme and SDD-1 (to be discussed later).

7.1 Concurrency.

There is an extensive literature of concurrency problems and solutions. This literature, excepting purely theoretical works, is of two basic types: operating system problems and database problems. One difference between them is that operating system work has dealt mostly with centralized systems under the assumption (usually implicit) that back-out (preemption; undo; transaction abort) is not available. Another difference is the granularity of concurrency: operating systems usually deal with resources used for a relatively long time (such as tape drives), or with moderately large objects (such as files and directories). The primary exception to this is internal tables, but we are more concerned with the synchronization features visible to a user of the system rather than those used in the system's construction. In databases concurrency control may be at the level of individual records or tuples. The finer granularity tends to result in different implementation techniques. Another difference between operating systems concurrency control and database concurrency control is that consideration of distributed concurrency problems seems to have occurred more in the database area, though there is increasing interest in distributed operating system problems.

7.1.1 General Approach.

As mentioned in Chapter 3, the two main approaches to concurrency control have been locking and timestamps. Our scheme is the first to use locking to support nested transactions; Reed's [Reed78] was the first to use timestamps to support nested transactions. Timestamp synchronization requires operations to (appear to) be performed in timestamp order; its correctness is easy to grasp. Locking insures serializability somewhat indirectly, through the two-phase locking rule. Each scheme has drawbacks and advantages relative to the other. Locking requires that there be an instant in time at which a transaction holds all the locks it ever needs. In contrast, timestamp synchronization does not require that all of a transaction's resources be held at once. These facts suggest that in some circumstances timestamp synchronization might provide more concurrency. However, consider also the following contrast. Locking permits transactions to serialize only as necessary and "find" a place relative to other transactions dynamically. Timestamp synchronization determines the relative order of transactions in advance. It would appear that timestamp schemes require additional waiting (to know that no more transactions with timestamps in a certain range will arrive at a given node) or will abort more transactions (a transaction with an early timestamp may not be runnable at a given node because a transaction with a later timestamp has already committed). Bernstein, Shipman, and Wong

[BSW79] have examined different methods of insuring serializability. Their formal analysis indicates that timestamping may provide more concurrency than two-phase locking. However, their paper investigates concurrency without examining other effects such as waiting, deadlock, and the number of transactions aborted. Another discussion of timestamp protocols in distributed systems may be found in [BG80b].

Two of the principal architects of the SDD-1 system (which uses timestamps) have written a report [BG80a] evaluating a number of concurrency control mechanisms within a particular model. They arrived at the conclusion that no single scheme of the large number that they examined was best for all situations. They were able to identify a small number of schemes as definitely better than the rest, and called these *dominant* methods. Some of the dominant methods used two-phase locking. However, different choices for various system parameters could make each of the dominant methods better than the others under some circumstances. We conclude that our choice of two-phase locking is neither universally good nor universally bad. One interesting thing about the report is that the authors suggest some novel combinations of timestamp and lock methods. A difference between their model and ours is that they were considering replication of objects at different nodes.

Of late, increased concurrency through the use of multiple versions of data has been investigated. As we will see, this is a feature of Reed's scheme. The idea is to allow database reads to get a consistent, though possibly slightly out of date, view of the world, and reduce conflicts between reads and writes. Some papers in this area include [BG82, PK82, and Silberschatz82].

In addition to the distinction between locking and timestamps, concurrency control may be distributed or centralized. Garcia-Molina [Garcia-Molina79] has investigated the theoretical performance of both centralized and distributed locking in some detail. He indicates that the simplicity of centralized locking and the lower total number of messages required (compared with distributed schemes) make centralized locking attractive. Centralized locking may also help avoid deadlocks and prevent bottlenecks at locks because it has more information at hand to make better decisions than are possible with a distributed algorithm. Two drawbacks of centralized locking are that the central lock manager represents a potential system bottleneck and that it is "weak link" in terms of failures. For the latter reason it is important that another node can take over the lock management function if the current lock manager fails. Garcia-Molina presents an algorithm for a new node to pick up where a (supposedly) crashed lock manager left off. See also [Garcia-Molina82] for more on distributed election techniques. We feel Garcia-Molina's algorithm and correctness arguments are more complex than ours.

7.1.2 Replication.

Our scheme does not deal inherently with multiple copies of objects (replicated objects). We suggest that replication be built on top of a transaction system, as Gifford [Gifford79] has done. Building replication this way seems to lead to a simpler system structure. A number of schemes have included replication in the base level design, e.g., Distributed INGRES [Stonebraker79], SDD-1 [BSRG77], and Sirius-Delta [LeLann81]. It is argued that while building replication in at the lowest level does complicate the system design, the resulting system may exhibit performance advantages over the two-level design. This argument has not yet been conclusively verified or refuted.

In addition to differences in the level at which replication is introduced, the schemes mentioned above present a variety of concurrency control mechanisms for accessing the various copies. SDD-1 uses timestamps, as does a scheme suggested by Thomas [Thomas79]. Thomas uses majority consensus voting by the copies of the objects. SDD-1 adopted some of Thomas' ideas, but uses a unique and complicated concurrency control scheme involving pre-analysis of transaction classes and four different protocols for different cases. Gifford uses locking instead of timestamps, but does use majority consensus similar to Thomas' scheme. However, Gifford generalized Thomas' "one site, one vote" rule to weighted voting.

Garcia-Molina's report [Garcia-Molina79] presents a number of different methods for processing updates to a replicated distributed data base. He concludes that centralized locking may promise better performance than a distributed voting algorithm such as Thomas' or Gifford's, at least in a number of interesting cases. On the other hand, it cannot yet be said that one method or the other has a strong advantage.

7.1.3 Deadlock.

Deadlock has been studied extensively and many schemes have been designed for preventing, avoiding, and detecting deadlocks, for both centralized and distributed systems. We mentioned several related papers in Chapter 6: Obermarck's scheme [Obermarck80] is fairly close to ours, and Menasce and Muntz's paper [MM79] is also related. Goldman's thesis [Goldman77] seems to be the most similar, though. Both Goldman and Obermarck present convincing schemes, complete with proofs. Menasce and Muntz's scheme does not work, as was pointed out by Gligor and Shattuck [GS80]. Though the details of our basic scheme are slightly different from Goldman's and Obermarck's, the main novelty of our algorithm for distributed deadlock detection lies in the extension to nested transactions, which involves some significant subtleties as was pointed out in Chapter 6. For further information on deadlock, Isloor and Marsland's article [IM80] may be useful; it is a good introduction to the topic and includes a convenient annotated bibliography. Another bibliography on deadlock is available as [Zobel83].

It should be noted that we are not dealing with the most general cases of resource allocation and deadlock handling: not only do we restrict transactions to await only one resource at a time, we deal with only one kind of resource (read/write locks). Generalization may not be overly difficult, but our approach may become less attractive in some respects. In particular, most generalizations seem to introduce more aborting of transactions not actually involved in a deadlock. Gligor and Shattuck [GS80] discuss this issue. Generalization was discussed in Chapter 6, and more will be said in Chapter 8.

7.1.4 Granularity.

The work done at IBM [Gray79] is representative of centralized system solutions to concurrency control; more recently they have been extending that research to distributed systems [Lindsay79, Lindsay84, Williams81]. The Xerox work [LS, IMS78, Paxton79, SMB79] shows a slightly different approach in that it has been oriented towards distributed file systems, while the IBM research has concentrated on databases. Although many of the same problems arise and the conceptual approaches to them can be similar, the specific solutions to the problems tend to be different in the two domains. This derives mainly from the fact that file systems are simpler than databases in both structure and consistency constraints. Also, file system locking is generally based on physical memory structure (i.e., one locks files or pages) rather than logical pieces (records, indexes), which is more typical of databases. The difference in granularity of locking between databases and file systems is not intrinsic, and is perhaps not important. For example, file systems can certainly be built with finer grained locking (e.g., ranges of bytes in a file). However, Gray [Gray75] believes that variable granularity of locking is important in database applications. System R is the only system we know of that provides variable granularity. Gray [Gray80b] says that variable granularity of locks was quite effective in System R.

There might be substantial technical problems in achieving high performance with fine granularity using the methods we have suggested in earlier chapters, because of the per-object overhead. Still, the difficulty of the problems depends on the level of performance required, and a straightforward implementation might suffice in many cases. We will say a little more about implementation in the next chapter. For more information on granularity, [Carey83, Korth81, Korth82a, Korth82b] may be helpful.

7.2 Reliability.

While many operating systems have included some means for backing up files to avoid catastrophe, these systems have generally not provided consistency sufficient for database systems. Hence the more relevant reliability work has been done mainly in the area of databases [Verhofstad78], though the two fields seem to be merging as in concurrency.

Our solutions to reliability problems are not original. Building permanent storage using logs is well known, and is described nicely in [Gray78]. Lampson and Sturgis [LS] have described a method for constructing a reliable disk storage system using current technology magnetic disks. Checksumming and retransmission of messages are certainly not new techniques. The two-phase commit protocol has also been around for a while, and has been incorporated in many designs.

Almost all distributed schemes have used two-phase commit to achieve consistency across multiple nodes. The reliability mechanism proposed by Hammer and Shipman

[HS80] for SDD-1[1] takes a somewhat different approach: it provides the illusion of global time and guarantees delivery of certain kinds of messages. Their design is called the *RelNet* (for *reliable network*). The RelNet is built in a number of layers and uses logical and real time in innovative ways. The algorithms are complex, and the correctness arguments are quite subtle and involved. The RelNet approach was taken in order to avoid certain delays possible when a crash occurs at an inconvenient point of the two-phase commit protocol. Most implementations of two-phase commit have this problem. Further, most schemes will not survive permanent failure of a node, either. Byzantine agreement, discussed briefly in Chapter 3, solves both problems.

In contrast with two-phase commit and Byzantine agreement, the RelNet employs a scheme of primary and backup nodes, similar to Distributed INGRES, discussed below. In the RelNet, if any of the primary or backup nodes for a given transaction fail, they may not be used again. If a sequence of single failures occurs over time, then we may be left with only one backup. If the last backup fails, the scheme breaks down. See [HS80] for the details.

7.3 Both Concurrency and Reliability.

Many people have recognized that concurrency control and recovery aspects of a system must be coordinated to preserve consistency in the face of failures, and a number of schemes have been devised that address both concurrency and reliability problems in single-level transaction systems. In this section we examine a number of such schemes and compare them one on one with our proposed design. Nested transaction designs are described in a later section.

---

1. SDD-1, as originally formulated, had no reliability mechanism.

7.3.1 Distributed INGRES.

It is hard to compare our scheme with Stonebraker's Distributed INGRES [Stonebraker79] because he implements several mechanisms all at once: concurrency control, recovery, and replication. His scheme involves (reliably) keeping track of which nodes are up and down, and assumes that messages arrive in the order sent. His design has difficulty handling communications failures that *partition* the network, i.e., divide the network into two or more disjoint sets of nodes that can communicate to other nodes in their subset, but not with nodes in other subsets. Our scheme handles network partitions. The design of Distributed INGRES is based on assumptions as to what operations are most common; i.e., its performance is optimized for a particular class of behaviors. Our design is not based on as many assumptions of that kind.

Stonebraker also suggests a way to trade reliability off against performance: one varies the number of backups for the coordinator of a transaction. The overhead of transaction processing in Distributed INGRES is partly proportional to the number of backups. However, reliability is enhanced with more backups, because the system continues to work correctly unless the coordinator and all backups fail. Our design has chosen a particular level of reliability and is not adjustable the way Stonebraker's design is. However, because of the difference in methods by which reliability is achieved in the two schemes, it is possible that his design is more costly for the same degree of reliability.

7.3.2 SDD-1.

The RelNet (discussed above) proposed by Hammer and Shipman [HS80] for use with SDD-1, provides more functionality than our design: guaranteed message delivery, messages delivered in order, etc. These properties seem necessary to support SDD-1. In contrast, our design has built somewhat *ad hoc* mechanisms in the few places where features of this kind are needed. The performance characteristics of the RelNet algorithms could significantly decrease the performance of SDD-1.

Besides the reliability aspects of SDD-1, the concurrency aspects are also complicated and subtle. The actual synchronization algorithms (called P1, P2, P3, and P4) are straightforward. The difficult part is classifying transactions and building the tables that say which algorithm to apply in which cases. The point of the analysis and multiple synchronization algorithms is to achieve higher performance in certain cases assumed to be most common. In this sense SDD-1 depends on predictability of transactions. Knowledge of the data read and written by different (classes of) transactions is required in order to build the tables that permit the more efficient protocols P1, P2, and P3 to be used. P4 is an expensive protocol, but it must be used for any transaction not fitting into the predefined classes. If transactions are sufficiently predictable, SDD-1 may outperform our design. On the other hand, because of the expense of P4 synchronization, SDD-1 may not be attractive when transactions are not so predictable.

7.3.3 System R.

The System R database system project at IBM, San Jose, has produced a number of papers that we have already cited (e.g., [Gray78, Gray75, Gray79, Gray80a, Lindsay79]), both in this chapter and in earlier ones. System R uses locking similar to ours. However, the System R locking scheme additionally incorporates variable granularity of locks. It would be easy to extend our scheme with additional lock modes similar to those used in System R. What is more problematic is that the variable granularity scheme depends on a fixed organization of data objects into a hierarchy.[1] The problem is how to fit arbitrary user data types into the hierarchy, and how to insure that the hierarchical locking rules are enforced.

System R uses a log method for object state restoration. Gray describes the logging and recovery techniques in a fair amount of detail in [Gray78, Gray79, Gray81]. A distributed version of System R is under development [Lindsay84, Lindsay79, Williams81].

In [Gray81], it is mentioned that System R has a nested transaction mechanism that it uses internally. It is perhaps a bit restricted, but seems to support locking and recovery semantics similar to our design. However, the mechanism is not made available to users.

---

1. Gray [Gray78] describes how the design readily extends to arbitrary directed acyclic graphs.

7.3.4 DFS and the Paxton/WFS System.

Two distributed file systems that have been developed at the Xerox Palo Alto Research Center (PARC) are DFS [IMS78] (also known as Juniper), and a system by Paxton [Paxton79] built on top of WFS [SMB79]. The two systems provide very much the same capabilities: creation, reading, writing, updating, and deletion of files. Files are maintained only on *file servers*, which are dedicated to providing the file system function. Both systems preserve consistency by performing actions (mainly reads and writes of blocks of data within files) as part of (single-level) transactions that are committed (or aborted) atomically everywhere, and they achieve reliability through careful updating of disk storage and a two-phase commit protocol.

The main difference between the two schemes is that DFS file servers provide a higher level interface. DFS is implemented almost entirely in the servers, whereas the Paxton/WFS design slices the system at a different point, providing lower level functionality in the servers (WFS file system) and placing more of the functionality in the users of the system (the part developed by Paxton). Paxton discusses the advantages and disadvantages of this choice in where to place the functionality of the system. For our purposes, the two systems are quite comparable because they provide about the same features and level of reliability. Some assumptions have been made concerning communication (e.g., messages are delivered in order); these assumptions are justified because of properties of the hardware network used by the system (the Xerox Ethernet).

The papers are interesting because they provide substantial detail about actual implementations of reliable distributed subsystems, in contrast to our paper design and simulation. Gifford [Gifford79] has built a system providing replicated files on top of DFS; we say more about his work in Chapter 8.

7.3.5 Sirius-Delta.

Several papers [LeLann81, Boudenant81, BR81] describe the Sirius-Delta distributed real-time transaction processing system, a part of Project Sirius at INRIA. Sirius-Delta provides single-level transactions using read/write locking for concurrency control. Timestamps are used to break ties and choose deadlock victims. Deadlock avoidance is used rather than deadlock detection; hence undo because of transaction conflicts could be frequent. However, it is assumed that the amount of work to be redone is small because transactions are assumed to be short.

The system incorporates a novel technique for generating timestamps: a token is passed among the nodes. The token (an integer) is passed in a circle, called the *virtual ring*. When a node has the token, it may allocate some timestamps starting with the current value of the token. The token is incremented beyond the highest timestamp allocated before being sent to the next node in the virtual ring. This method insure fair allocation of timestamps to all nodes, provided the token circulates rapidly enough, etc.

The system also uses the virtual ring as part of its reliability mechanism - the set of nodes currently in the ring are the "up" nodes, and protocols are provided for eliminating failed nodes from the ring and for permitting recovered nodes to join the ring. Network partition is possible, but the data are replicated, and may be operated upon only if a majority of copies of each required datum is available, so partition does not break the system.

A novel version of two-phase commit is used to overcome single failures of nodes, including coordinator failure at any point in the protocol. A complex scheme of distributed logs completes the set of reliability mechanisms. Sirius-Delta is reasonably simple, particularly considering its functionality, and is a working system.

7.4 Nested Transactions.

The earliest paper describing the concept underlying what we call nested transactions seems to be [Davies73] (his term is *spheres of control*). Davies has written several papers describing his ideas, including a comprehensive one fairly recently [Davies78]. However, he seems to be more concerned with overall semantics than with implementation techniques, and considers even more generality than we have. For example, we assumed that results are never released before transaction commit, and Davies explores the semantics of early release. (Montgomery [Montgomery78] and Takagi [Takagi79] have designed systems including early release.)

Lomet [Lomet77] examines some aspects of incorporating recovery and synchronization ideas into programming languages. It appears that he might even have intended to handle nested atomic actions. However his scheme is for a centralized system and does not address the issues involved in distribution or processor crashes.

7.4.1 Reed's Design

Reed's thesis [Reed78] is the first detailed scheme dealing with nested transactions, and it describes a distributed system. It is the combination of his arrangement of pseudo-times and dependent commit records that implements nested transactions. He also introduces the notion of multiple versions of objects. Assuming that only one version of each object is kept, then it is not too hard to compare our scheme with his. Reed's pseudo-times are essentially timestamps. These timestamps readily resolve (avoid) deadlocks. However our scheme will result in fewer needless transaction aborts, because we use deadlock detection instead of deadlock avoidance (see the discussion in Chapter 6).

Reed's basic scheme permits transaction starvation: a transaction request that performs updates can be aborted every time it is run. If a transaction reads any objects written later by another transaction with an earlier pseudo-time (i.e., the read and write are attempted in an order opposite to that of the pseudo-times for the transactions), the transaction with the earlier pseudo-time will abort because it cannot acquire needed objects at its particular pseudo-time. To help solve this problem Reed introduces token reservations, which amount to pre-allocation of resources, a deadlock prevention technique. But token reservations require a certain amount of predictability, and can reduce concurrency. The reliability mechanisms of our scheme and his are comparable.

When more than one object version is kept, Reed's design can achieve better performance in an environment where there are many read-only requests and relatively few updates, but updates may affect many objects. The difference is that the read-only requests would be held up in our scheme because of the locks held by the long running update transactions, whereas those read-only transactions would just use slightly older (but consistent) data in Reed's system. Chapter 6 mentioned some recent papers that discuss multiple version techniques.

In sum, Reed has solved much the same problem as we have, and each of the two schemes has advantages that may make it more attractive in certain application environments. It would be interesting to implement both schemes and compare their efficiency.

7.4.2 The Argus Project

The Argus project [Liskov79, Liskov82, LS83, LM83] is planned to incorporate a substantial implementation of nested transactions. Their design is quite similar to ours, since our research was part of the Argus project. However, we have aimed for a simple design, to aid in conveying the concepts of nested transaction to a broad audience, whereas the Argus team is building an actual system.

Here is a brief summary of the differences between our design and Argus, as we currently understand it. Argus does not permit a parent to execute concurrently with a child transaction, but does allow the parent to acquire locks. In Argus, an *independent* top level transaction may be spawned by *any* transaction, to achieve a permanent effect, regardless of the success of the spawning transaction. Argus incorporates a scheme for detecting and eliminating orphan transactions before they can perceive any non-serializable situations. While these points of difference are not trivial, they do not significantly affect the intended semantics of nested transaction processing.

It should also be noted that Argus deals with detailed semantics of communication, and goes beyond most distributed system designs in that it is specifying a language as well as a system. The Argus language is based upon CLU [Liskov81].

7.4.3 LOCUS

LOCUS [Popek81, WP83] is a distributed operating system built by a team at UCLA. It is based upon UNIX[1] and targeted to a local area network communication substrate. Recently a nested transaction mechanism for it was described [MMP83]. In this scheme a UNIX process is used for each transaction (top-level or inferior), and locking is on the basis of UNIX files. The locking rules are straight from [Moss81]. State restoration is also based on our design. However, commitment and reliability mechanisms are somewhat different from ours, though still based on a two-phase commit protocol. The LOCUS project is explicitly concerned with continuing operation during network partitions, and allows replicates to diverge, with automatic or manual merging performed when the partition no longer exists. Thus, while LOCUS incorporates some of our ideas, it does not entirely adhere to our philosophy of consistency.

7.4.4 Clouds

There is a team at Georgia Tech developing a distributed operating system called Clouds [MAT83, Allchin83]. They have been investigating application of nested transaction concepts to distributed operating systems and application running under such systems. While the semantics we have pursued have been more like traditional database systems, Clouds is extending nested transaction to such objects as semaphores, queues, and directories. It will allow some forms of communication among top-level (and non-top-level) transactions through such system defined data types, and possibly through user defined types as well.

---

1. UNIX is a trademark of Bell Laboratories.

7.4.5 Eden

Eden [Lazowska81] is an object oriented distributed system project at the University of Washington. The file system design [Jessop82] includes nested transactions. It implements the nesting in an interesting way: an inferior transaction operates on its parent as a data object. In this way the parent's versions of modified data will be obtained, etc. This is an interesting duality of transactions and data. The current version of EDEN is built on top of UNIX and suffers a noticeable performance penalty, which could be greatly improved with redesign. Unfortunately, as of this writing, EDEN does not yet support nested transactions.

7.4.6 Cells

A team at Ohio State University is using nested transactions in the construction of a distributed operating system called Cells [LL83]. Unlike most of the other projects building nested transactions, Cells does not provide transactions to the user. Rather, nested transaction techniques are used inside the operating system to improve its resiliency. Since nested transaction will be used only in particular ways, some aspects may be streamlined, and some problems need not be solved because they never arise. For example, Cells does not need sophisticated mechanisms for resolving orphans because of the manner in which activity is stylized and restricted.

7.5 Summary.

Because few distributed transaction systems have been implemented and there is no performance data, no cogent comparisons of distributed transaction schemes can be made. Further, there is not even agreement on the criteria on which to base such comparisons. Therefore, we have simply enumerated the differences in features supported by a number of other schemes.

As can be seen, a number of projects are investigating implementation of nested transactions, in a variety of settings, and in general or specific contexts. However, because the concept is still new, and many of the projects are incomplete, it is too early to draw any conclusions. We speculate that nested transactions will be a useful structuring tool for systems and applications work making significant use of concurrency or recovery management features. That is, nested transactions may help organize a system and simplify it. In the next chapter we will comment further and describe why we think nested transactions simplify design and implementation of distributed systems.

8. Discussion.

In this chapter we summarize the accomplishments of our work, attempt to relate it to significant concepts of computer science, and indicate areas for further research.

8.1 Summary of Accomplishments.

We have presented a high-level design of a nested transaction system for a distributed computing environment that can achieve high reliability. The presentation proceeded in a number of stages.

In Chapter 2 we made explicit the underlying assumptions concerning hardware and its failure properties. We defined what we mean by a distributed system: a group of *nodes* communicating by sending *messages*. A node consists of three components: a *processor*, some *volatile* memory, the contents of which are lost in crashes, and some *permanent* memory, whose contents survive crashes. We described a model of failure in which behaviors are of three kinds: *good* (normal), *tolerable* (recoverable failures), and *intolerable* (non-recoverable failures). We *assume* that intolerable behaviors never occur. That assumption is reasonable because we carefully insure that the probability of intolerable behavior can be made arbitrarily small by increasing the redundancy of the system.[1]

Having explored the physical foundations, in Chapter 3 we turned to the semantics of transaction processing. We introduced the concepts *internal consistency*, *external consistency*, and *congruity*. We suggested *serializability* as a (partial) means for achieving consistency in the face of concurrent processing, and described the usual two-phase locking method for insuring serializability. Having dealt with concurrency, we then turned our attention to handling failures. To do so, we introduced the idea of transaction *abort*, and object *state restoration* as a means for achieving it. Locking and state restoration were sufficient for local consistency, but a distributed commit protocol, such as the well known

---

1. The one place where we fail to meet this requirement, neglecting issues of software reliability, is the lack of a checkpointing mechanism. For discussion of this issue, see Chapter 4 and the suggestion for further work later in this chapter.

two-phase commit protocol, or Byzantine agreement, was required for global consistency. We discussed briefly the congruity problems inherent in physical input/output.

Having described a single-level distributed transaction system, we proceeded to extend that scheme to nested transactions in Chapters 4, 5, and 6. Chapter 4 discussed the concepts and motivation for nested transactions, and the extended locking and state restoration algorithms. In Chapter 5 we presented the transaction management algorithm. The purpose of that algorithm is to insure that every transaction is eventually committed or aborted as it should be. However, the version of the algorithm given in Chapter 5 did not handle deadlock situations: these were the topic of Chapter 6. There we not only presented a novel distributed deadlock detection algorithm, but we also showed how simple but careful use of the idea of transaction *priorities* can insure eventual success of each transaction request (provided failures are not too frequent, of course).

In Chapter 7 we mentioned a number of related works. Though many of our algorithms derive from these works, the extensions to nested transactions are new. The only prior work to deal with nested transactions in as much detail is Reed's thesis [Reed78]. Our design has advantages over his if his system is restricted to retaining only one version of each object. If multiple versions are kept, then Reed's design can be superior in some situations, and the desirability of our scheme over his would be based in part upon the likelihood of those situations. We believe that our approach (locking and state restoration) is more easily generalized than the timestamp approach followed by Reed and others. We say more about possible generalizations later in this chapter.

In sum, the main contributions of our work are the locking, state restoration, transaction management, and deadlock detection algorithms for distributed nested transactions. With a few caveats, we have presented a design for a system providing reliable processing of nested transactions in a distributed environment. We have dealt effectively with the problems of concurrency and reliability, culminating with a guarantee of progress within the system that is about as strong as possible. Our design is a bit unusual in that it is not specifically oriented towards providing a distributed data base or file system. Instead the design was directed towards general purpose programming.

The locking and state restoration concepts are our most significant and fundamental contribution. The distributed transaction manager and deadlock detector do not extend previous work very much. However, we feel that it was important to show that distributed transaction management, and deadlock detection (and avoidance), can be designed for nested transactions. The particular algorithms are oriented more to illustration of possibilities, issues, and problems than to actual implementation. We stress that the important aspect of the research is the concept of nested transactions rather than the details of our scheme.

8.2 The Broader Context.

We have presented a new (but not original) concept, nested transactions, and have described one way of building a system providing that concept. Now we would like to relate nested transactions to the whole of computer science and software engineering. The most obvious connections are with databases and operating systems, with concurrency and recovery. However, those subject areas are not paradigms or theories, but application and problem domains. What nested transactions do is apply the paradigm of *hierarchy* to those problem areas in a new way. In this section we explore the notion of hierarchy. Our main goal in this exploration is to convey why we believe nested transactions are a useful innovation. A secondary aim is to find ways in which our use of hierarchy can be extended to improve nested transactions in interesting ways.

The common usage of the word *hierarchy* refers to a system of classification or stratification, especially as found in government, the military, and religious organizations. This leads naturally to some uses of hierarchy in computer science: levels of detail, of grouping, of responsibility. Hierarchy is also used frequently in the narrower sense of organizations formally equivalent to trees (the data structure, not the plant). Let us briefly mention some of the more notable application of hierarchy in computer science, and hardware and software engineering.

In hardware a physical hierarchy of detail, design, and construction is apparent. Working from the bottom to the top we have silicon doping, electron devices, integrated circuits, boards, subsystems, computers, and multi-computer networks. Each level in this hierarchy embodies different design techniques and theories. Thus, judicious use of hierarchy permits separation of concerns. The kind of hierarchy that occurs in hardware pervades engineering. One is not surprised to see similar techniques and philosophies used in analog electronics such as televisions and radios. However engineering hierarchy is quite apparent in mechanical devices, too. Prime examples are vehicles, from motorcycles and automobiles through ships and spacecraft. One finds assemblies and sub-assemblies, often independently designed, though of course intended to work together harmoniously.

Returning to more familiar ground, hierarchy is used many different ways in software. Two obvious examples are hierarchical file systems, and nesting of structures in programming languages. A more subtle use of hierarchy can be found in software design techniques, especially top-down design. Of course a hierarchical design method leads naturally to hierarchically organized programs. However, some uses of hierarchy in software are not directly related to design or coding techniques. In particular, hierarchical data structures are used for sorting. Similar applications of hierarchy in database and operating systems include hierarchically organized indexes, hierarchies of lock modes, and hierarchies of locks on larger and larger groups of objects. On a grander scale, we see hierarchy suggested in the construction of abstract data types and in layered operating systems. There is obvious hierarchy in layered network protocols.

Why is hierarchy so pervasive in engineering and computer science? What makes it so useful? We believe that the key property of hierarchy is that it allows large and complex structures to be grasped, designed, and built without their having to be understood as a whole. Rather, each piece of the structure is related only to a few other pieces: ones in the layer above, in the layer below, and in the same layer, and by no means to all elements in any layer. We speculate that one reason minimal connections make design easier is the limited capacity of human short term memory, and human reasoning capability in general. But even if a machine could be used to do the design, as the number of connections to each component grows, so grows the difficulty of analysis and design. More subtle effects of increased connectivity include higher cost of design changes, and the possibility of increased likelihood of failure. In sum, low connectivity leads to simplicity and manageability.

Nested transactions as we have described them provide a strict hierarchy (tree) of transactions. Now one may argue the point of whether top-level transactions root separate hierarchies, or if we can conceive of a global "super-transaction" that pulls all transactions into a single hierarchy.[1] However, the point we wish to make is that nested transactions conform to trees, and not to layers. Perhaps one of the most interesting extensions of nested transactions would be to introduce layering, too. An analogy with programming languages will better illustrate what we mean. Consider an Algol-like language, in which the nesting of procedures produces a hierarchy. Nested transactions are very similar to that procedural hierarchy. Both tree structures represent ever larger groupings of primitive operations. True layering is achieved when one adds abstract data types, as, for example, in CLU. Rather than simply grouping primitives together, one now can build new kinds of objects, essentially adding more primitives to (on top of) the existing ones.

Maybe nested transaction can be extended in that way. But even as they stand, nested transactions allow hierarchical design principles, and the advantages of hierarchical thought, to be applied to the construction of transaction-oriented applications. The hierarchy of procedures and data types, and the use of top-down design, are all nice, but the concurrency, and maybe more importantly, the recovery features of nested transactions enhance our ability to build workable systems. This is why we feel nested transactions are advantageous even if they offer no performance improvement, or even limited performance degradation.

8.3 Suggestions for Further Work.

There are many interesting areas for further investigation. Below we discuss a number of such topics in turn.

1. We believe that each view, single or separate hierarchies, has its use, especially when trying to formalize aspects of nested transactions.

8.3.1 Language Design.

We have generally ignored the question of integrating the semantics and mechanism of any system supporting transactions into a programming language. The recovery block approach [RLT78, Lomet77] gives a start. The Argus project [Liskov79, Liskov82, etc.] is investigating this area. The problem is challenging because not only must the concurrency and recovery aspects be incorporated into the language design, but one must also devise an acceptable model of distributed computing that can be expressed nicely in a programming language. There has yet to be a complete model of reliable distributed computation, including the details of processing that we omitted (such as user-level communications, and process structure). Should such a semantic model be formulated, the task of designing a language around it will still be very difficult. We are not yet to the stage where individual language feature proposals can be evaluated, not the least because definitive criteria on which to base such judgments are lacking. However, attempts are being made to define and discuss the issues (e.g., [LM83]).

Here are some of the issues that must be resolved. What are objects? Are they replicated? If so, fully are partially? Do they have multiple versions? Is state restoration automatic? If not, how is it expressed by the user? What level of concurrency is permitted or achieved? How is potential concurrency expressed? For example, is concurrency implicit or do programmers write a number of sequential processes that execute in parallel? How is inter-node communication presented to the programmer? Do synchronization and state restoration apply to all objects? If not, how are non-atomically accessed objects handled? These questions are just samples of the questions that need to be answered.

8.3.2 Implementation.

Going beyond the semantic and language design issues, there are a number of interesting questions of implementation. A particularly interesting subject is the organization of objects in volatile and permanent memory and their movement between the two. The main challenge seems to be to achieve high performance with an automatic system. See [Svobodova80] and [Arens81] for some work on this problem. It is natural to implement Reed's multiple object versions with a log; he has discussed how to do that in [Reed78].

In addition to the organization and updating of memory, there are a number of questions concerning communication. For example, it must be decided how to packetize messages and re-assemble them, should the need arise. How should receiver buffering and flow control be performed, if at all? Is any low level sequence numbering, acknowledgment, or retransmission scheme required to achieve the basic level of reliability sufficient for our protocols? That is, we have not assumed the highest reliability, but we have assumed failures to be relatively rare; some systems may find it desirable to use low level reliability protocols to reduce the amount of work redone as a result of higher level transaction aborts.

We did not supply the details of organization and format of the various tables that transaction management requires. We also did not describe exactly how to abort running transactions - an operation that depends on the model of computation used. But in addition to the question of techniques, there are subtle questions of tuning performance. For example, there are several places where our algorithms retransmit various messages. How can one intelligently choose the interval between transmissions?

We briefly described a number of projects in Chapter 7, and they just begin to scratch the surface of the issues involved.

8.3.3 Checkpointing.

As we explained in Chapter 4, our scheme has one vulnerability to failure that we did not fix. If a top-level transaction runs for a long time, it becomes increasingly likely that its node will crash, aborting the entire transaction. We pointed out that a checkpointing mechanism is required if transactions may run long enough for node crashes to reduce reliability below the desired level. We also mentioned that designing a checkpointing mechanism requires elaborating a model of transaction execution in considerable detail.

One approach that does not depend on the semantics of transaction execution very much is to save the entire state of a node periodically. This could be done by just stopping normal processing for a moment and writing copies of all modified pages to permanent memory. Unfortunately, local checkpoints are not sufficient because of communication between nodes. If checkpoints of different nodes are not properly coordinated, a domino-effect can result, making the checkpoints worthless. Russell has examined this particular problem in some detail [Russell80]. By keeping track of the flow of messages in the system, it might be possible to coordinate checkpoints and arrive at a workable scheme. In addition to taking the checkpoints in the first place, there is also the problem of unwinding them all correctly in case of failure. Some progress has been made in this area by researchers at IBM [SY84].

A different approach is to checkpoint individual transactions. One advantage of this approach is that the completion of a transaction at the end of two-phase commit is also a checkpoint for that transaction, beyond which the transaction will never back up. A further advantage is that the amount of checkpointing work might be much less than checkpointing nodes, because one would checkpoint only those transactions that have been running for a relatively long time. But as pointed out before, this approach requires a much more detailed and constrained model of transaction execution. We have presented some preliminary work along these lines [Moss83].

8.3.4 Aborting Running Transactions.

Because our algorithms do not require a transaction to wait for its children to finish before aborting, we introduced the possibility of orphans. Even if we made transactions wait to abort, crashes could still generate orphans. The transaction management algorithm allows us to find orphans and decide that they should be aborted. However, we did not explain exactly how to abort an orphan. The details of aborting a running transaction are very implementation dependent, but here are some techniques that might be useful.

First, we can try waiting for the orphan to get to the *finished* state and abort it then. Presumably aborting then presents no problems (we have assumed so all along); it should be simple since activity pertaining to the transaction has supposedly stopped. If we get tired of waiting, it always works to simulate a crash of the node on which the orphan is running. Naturally that technique should be used as a last resort, since it will tend to interfere with other activities, e.g., it may also create more orphans (at other nodes).

Waiting and simulating crashes are techniques that can always be applied, but waiting does not always work, and crashing is a bit heavy-handed and may generate more orphans. Here are two additional techniques that might work, depending on the details of the implementation. One possible approach is to undo everything associated with the transaction, release all the locks, and give failure returns to any further attempts to use the transaction id. That method works only if the user programs have absolutely no way of continuing to access objects they previously locked. The second technique is this: if use of a transaction id is restricted to a single process, then it may work to kill off that process. All user programs must then be designed to tolerate arbitrary disappearance of processes; we are not sure how easy or difficult that would be.

In sum, getting rid of orphans once they are found is a challenging problem. Entirely satisfactory solutions are implementation dependent and might not be possible. Further investigation of the problem is in order.

An alternative to getting rid of orphans is preventing them. This could be done by insuring that a parent transaction could never be discarded by a crash, causing foreign children to become orphans. We would need to guarantee that certain transactions would survive crashes. This requires a transaction checkpointing mechanism, such as that described in the previous section. For reasonable performance it also requires the ability to write to stable storage quickly, so that a checkpoint can be made rapidly just before a foreign child is created. Interestingly enough, fast stable storage has been designed and built [Needham83, BBP83]. Hence it may be possible to build a system that entirely avoids orphans. The disadvantage to such schemes are that the transactions that formerly were orphans must now wait for the crashed site to recover in some cases, before resources can be released. A still running child can be aborted to free its resources, but the transactions whose homes are the crashed site cannot be resolved until after recovery.

8.3.5 Higher Concurrency.

Our initial model of locking (in Chapter 4) permitted only exclusive access to objects. We extended that to include read-mode (shared) access almost immediately. Read/write locking is a compromise: it permits sufficient concurrency for many applications, and has relatively simple semantics. However, the semantics of read/write locking do not necessarily mesh well with the operations on objects. The generalization that seems to be desired is synchronization appropriate to each data type.

Directories provide a fairly typical example of a data type for which read/write locking is not always appropriate. For example, suppose one transaction is creating a new file in a particular directory. That operation clearly modifies the directory, and under our read/write locking scheme the transaction would have to wait for exclusive access to the directory object, and once it acquired the object, it would lock out all other transactions until it committed. However, it is sufficient to lock out just the transactions whose outcome will be different depending on whether the transaction succeeds or fails. Reed [Reed78] discusses ways to exploit particular kinds of object semantics to increase concurrency within his system design.

Montgomery's polyvalues [Montgomery78] provide a new approach to increasing concurrency: one calculates all the possible answers. In the case of the example given above, his scheme would perform two computations: one to calculate the result if the new file is created and the other to calculate the result if the file is not created. If there are n transactions updating the object, then we have the potential for up to 2^n polyvalues for any transaction using the object. The hope is that whether the individual file exists or not will not make any difference to most transactions, so though several values are calculated, the results are the same, and the transaction can commit regardless.

This is somewhat different from Takagi's scheme [Takagi79], where one basically assumes that all transactions will commit (without modifying the object any more). If the assumption later proves to be wrong, the tentative transactions are undone and recomputed. Both Montgomery and Takagi are applying corrective action after the fact, though in somewhat different ways. They also depend on the system to act in certain ways with high probability, or else they will perform worse than our scheme rather than better. The reason is that we merely reduce concurrency, whereas they actually perform multiple computations in some cases.

A middle ground would be to permit concurrent updates to the same object provided we could guarantee that they do not interfere with each other. While System R [Gray78] does not do this, it achieves a similar effect through variable granularity of locking: individual records of the database can be locked, even though they are embedded in larger data structures such as relations and files, which can themselves be locked. This requires care when records or tuples are to be created or deleted from a file or relation - we must make sure that no transaction has explicitly or implicitly depended upon the existence or non-existence of a given record.

The directory example provides an illustration of the kind of problem involved. Suppose that while our transaction that is creating a file is still running, another transaction attempts to list the directory. If it includes the new file, it will be wrong if the file creating transaction aborts or deletes the file. Similarly, if the listing transaction does not include the new file, it will be wrong if the file creating transaction commits. However, there is nothing at all wrong about letting two transactions writing files with different names to proceed concurrently. The point is that we must know how much and which part of the state of the directory is depended upon by each transaction. One of the subtleties is that some transactions implicitly depend on what is *not* part of the directory, too. For example, a directory listing not only asserts what files are part of a given directory, but also implicitly states what files are *not* in the directory (by not listing them). This latter property is what gives rise to so called *phantom records* in databases [EGLT76].

Something akin to the predicate locks of [EGLT76] can be used to decide when transactions must be blocked. It has been pointed out that computing general predicates is a hard problem. However, many collections of objects (stacks, queues, directories) require only simple predicates for their operations. Even general sets and relations can be handled by designing a suitable simplified class of predicates that are easy to check and calculate though perhaps not exact.

Instead of deriving predicates based on object states, one might achieve a more natural characterization by investigating the commutativity of different operations on objects of a given type. This is based on the fact that if two operations commute, and they are performed by different transactions, then there is no conflict between the transactions. Commutativity of read operations and non-commutativity of writes with either reads or other writes is the basis of read/write locking.

Korth has developed some theory related to generalized locking modes [Korth81].

However, he has considered the compatibility matrix, which defines which lock modes may be concurrently held by different transactions on the same object, to be given. Automatic or simplified derivation or specification of compatibility matrices for arbitrary data types would be an interesting extension of his work.

In addition to the control of concurrency among transactions for consistency reasons, we must be careful to insure exclusive access for the delicate parts of updates to many common data structures. That is, even though the elements of a set (say) are logically distinct, so that transaction-level concurrency control does not require synchronization, process-level synchronization may still be required when manipulating the physical data structure used to represent the set. However, the periods of time during which exclusive access of this kind is required are almost always brief, and the situation is comparatively well understood because of past experience with updating data structures in operating systems. A subtle point is that mutual exclusion may be required for undoing the work of aborted transactions. Also, if a process is killed off (because it is running on behalf of an orphan transaction, say) while it possesses a mutual exclusion lock, the integrity of the data structure can be destroyed.

If concurrent updates are allowed, the object state restoration techniques we employed in our design no longer work. It seems that the simple state-based approach must be replaced by a log-based method. One could use an undo log, as in [Gray78]. However, David Reed pointed out to us that it might be easier and safer[1] to use a *redo* log. A redo log would work as follows. Periodically we would save the state of the object; for purposes of argument, assume that the saved state is between updates. Then as updates are performed, we would record the operations executed so that we could re-execute them if desired. If one transaction aborted, we would fetch the saved state, and redo the operations of all *other* transactions (in order).

It is possible to take a new snapshot of the object even if there are updates for not yet committed transactions. However, doing so involves "imagining" (i.e., computing) what the

---

1. Redo is safer than undo because undo requires separate code that is complex and may be executed only rarely. It should be possible to use the normal "forward" executing code to perform redo.

object state would be if all the current pending updates aborted. Perhaps it would be easiest to keep two objects states: one is the current state and is what transactions actually manipulate; the second reflects only the committed updates. Doing things this way involves computing updates twice. However, if there are no pending updates, then the two object states will be the same and we can get away with performing the update only once. Thus, we expend more effort on high traffic items that tend to have pending updates, but get the original efficiency with low traffic items.

There is a trade-off between concurrency (delay) and processor time consumed. There is also the question of simplicity: the redo scheme is considered preferable because it is much easier to conceive of and implement general redo schemes than undo schemes, because for redo the user need not write extra code, whereas for undo the user must provide undo operations.

It is interesting to note that Montgomery's and Takagi's schemes also work automatically without extra user code. In some situations Montgomery's polyvalues might be the best approach, because results are held up only when they are actually different depending on whether or not some other transaction commits. Similarly, Takagi's scheme could be advantageous if aborts are relatively rare, as is usually the case. The schemes we have suggested hold a transaction up whenever its results *might* be different rather than when they are *actually* different. Optimistic concurrency control is an alternative to the schemes just discussed; it was described in Chapter 3.

Schemes that permit concurrent updates to the same object may have more trouble with checkpointing, because of the necessity for checkpointing to sample intermediate states. We note two other things in passing. First, if nested transactions could be extended with layers of abstraction, as discussed in the section on hierarchy, one might use such a mechanism to increase concurrency. The transaction- and process-level locking discussed above represent but two levels in a potentially many-layered hierarchy. Second, we note that we and others have been working on these ideas, but no results have been published at this time.

8.3.6 Communication.

The main shortcoming of our current design with respect to communication is that there is no integration of user communication primitives into the rest of the system. The reason it would be desirable to have such integration is that sending messages can permit information to flow outside of a transaction. If we stick to strict serializability semantics, recipients should not be able to actually receive and act on messages until the sending transaction has committed. It might appear that it is difficult to get a foreign node to do something, since the requesting transaction must commit before the foreign node can read the message, but then it is too late for the foreign node to perform acts with respect to the transaction. It seems that there must be some magic at the foreign node to cause a new process to be created as part of the transaction, or an old process to join the transaction, or something else of a similar nature. However, information is still restricted to flow only within a transaction until the transaction commits. Suitable semantics have yet to be worked out, much less implementation techniques to support them.

Reed [Reed78] has suggested permitting messages to flow and be received, but perhaps aborting dependent transactions that received results from aborted transactions. This is not unlike Takagi's scheme, in which one allows results to be read before they are committed, and then aborts the readers if the results are not actually committed. Such information-flow-based models bear some relationship to checkpointing as well, as we pointed out above.

As previously mentioned, the Argus design has a communication mechanism integrated with nested transactions [Liskov82, LM83, LS83]. Note that in Argus each user message invokes a foreign subtransaction.

8.3.7 Replication.

Several schemes attempt to provide multiple copy databases while simultaneously addressing concurrency and reliability problems. It is our feeling, seconded by Gifford [Gifford79], that it is easier, simpler, and more appropriate to implement replication on top of a system such as ours, so as to separate the issues of replication from the other problems. It may be true that better performance can be achieved by solving all problems simultaneously, but the result is considerably more complex. Also, an integrated solution will tend to be somewhat rigid in its approach to replication. That is, it would not be possible to implement a different replication algorithm without rearranging everything, whereas in the layered implementation we suggest, different replication algorithms could co-exist with no problem.

A number of algorithms have been proposed for performing replicated updates. Some have been based on timestamps (e.g., SDD-1 [BSRG77] and Distributed INGRES [Stonebraker79]) while others have been based on centralized locking (e.g., [Garcia-Molina79]). A whole variety of algorithms are examined, cataloged, and compared in general terms in a report by Bernstein and Goodman [BG80a]. Some of the schemes involve *voting*: in trying to acquire a replicated resource, one asks each copy if it is willing to go along with the request. If the transaction receives a quorum of agreeing votes, then it has the resource. The first voting algorithm was published by Thomas [Thomas79]. Gifford [Gifford79] presents an interesting generalization of voting: weighted votes.

We will not suggest what kind of replication scheme to use on top of our system. However, most replication schemes will permit work to proceed even when a few copies are unavailable. Such situations could be represented in our system as follows. Assuming a program has first gone through whatever protocol is required to insure exclusive access, one attempts to update all known (or available) copies, using a separate subtransaction for each update request. If enough of the subtransactions commit, then the overall update transaction can correctly commit; otherwise it must abort. The convenience is that the aborting happens automatically. One very simple approach is to start subtransactions doing the updates and commit the enclosing transaction if and only if at least a quorum of copies was updated. We believe the simplicity is a strong argument for this general method of implementing replication.

One problem that arises with replication is dealing with network partition. A partition is a failure that separates the communications network into two or more disjoint pieces no longer able to intercommunicate. The problem is that more than one partition may contain replicates of the same data, making inconsistent updates possible. Now one may simply rule out such accesses, by using majority (or weighted voting), but many argue that this is overly restrictive. Here are several papers on partition: [Brereton83, Wright83, WS83].

8.3.8 Multiple Versions.

We mentioned in the previous chapter that Reed's design [Reed78] incorporates the rather radical idea of keeping multiple versions of each object. These versions encode the entire history of an object's states, with global timestamps used to address the different versions. One need not keep all versions indefinitely - old versions can be discarded at will - only the latest version must be kept. If multiple version are deemed useful, it would be interesting to have a scheme that uses locking instead of (or more likely in combination with) timestamps to achieve a synthesis of Reed's design and ours. Such a combination seems strange now, but Bernstein and Goodman have suggested a number of schemes that mix locking and timestamping [BG80a]. Perhaps it would be possible to special case read-only transactions to achieve a simpler solution to the problem. Earlier we discussed some more recent work in this area [BG82, PK82, Silberschatz82].

8.3.9 Evaluation.

As noted in Chapter 7, there is no hard data available for comparing distributed transaction schemes, or even specific techniques. Some speculative works have been published (e.g., [BG80a, BSW79]), and a variety of claims have been made concerning different schemes. It would be very useful if experiments were performed comparing designs similar enough to each other to allow strong conclusions to be drawn. To make such comparisons well would require building two systems that are the same in all respects other than the mechanism or algorithm of interest. Hence, such cogent comparisons may never be possible.

An area in which experiments might be feasible is the handling of deadlock, because it is almost orthogonal to other system components in many designs (such as ours). It would be interesting to see comparisons of avoidance and detection within the same system under conditions of actual use. Another area in which experiments could probably be performed without too much effort is different schemes for object replication, if replication is built on top of an already existing transaction system.

8.4 Conclusions.

Transactions have been shown to be a useful tool for thinking about and constructing reliable distributed systems, because they provide a solid semantic foundation that has a simple interface. Once transaction processing has been provided, it is much easier to build the application system on top because the reliability and concurrency problems are already solved and may be mostly ignored. Nested transactions provide an interesting extension to single-level transaction semantics, by utilizing hierarchy, a powerful and pervasive design and engineering paradigm. We expect that transactions, and possibly nested transactions, will become the method of choice for building a wide variety of computing systems, especially distributed systems, because they make it easier to build such systems and to believe in them.

References

[Allchin83] J. E. Allchin, "An Architecture for Reliable Decentralized Systems", Ph.D. Thesis, School of Info. and Comp. Sci., Georgia Inst. of Tech., Sept. 1983.

[Arens81] Gail Arens, "Recovery of the Swallow Repository", S.M. Thesis, M.I.T. Dept. of Elec. Eng. and Comp. Sci., available as M.I.T. Lab. for Comp. Sci. Technical Report 252, Jan. 1981.

[BBP83] J. P. Banatre, M. Banatre, and F. Ployette, "Construction of a System Supporting Atomic Actions", *Proc. 3rd IEEE Symp. on Reliability in Distributed Software and Database Systems*,Clearwater Beach, Fla., Oct. 1983, pp. 95-99.

[BG80a] Philip A. Bernstein, Nathan Goodman, "Fundamental Algorithms for Concurrency Control in Distributed Database Systems", Computer Corp. of America Technical Report CCA-80-05, Feb. 1980.

[BG80b] P. A. Bernstein and N. Goodman, "Timestamp-Based Algorithms for Concurrency Control in Distributed Database Systems", *Proc. 6th Int'l Conf. on Very Large Data Bases*, Montreal, Canada, Oct. 1980.

[BG82] P. A. Bernstein and N. Goodman, "Concurrency Control Algorithms for Multiversion Database Systems", *ACM SIGACT-SIGOPS Symp. on Prin. of Distributed Computing*, Ottawa, Canada, Aug. 18-20, 1982, pp. 209-215.

[Boudenant81] J. Boudenant, "Some Solutions for Database Recovery in SIRIUS-DELTA", *Proc. 2nd Seminar in Distributed Data Sharing Systems*, Amsterdam, 1981.

[BR81] J. Boudenant and P. Rolin, "Modeling of the Transaction Distribution Algorithm in SIRIUS-DELTA", *Proc. IEEE Symp. on Reliability in Distributed Software and Database Systems*, Pittsburgh, July 21-22 1981, pp. 169-176.

[BRGP78] P. A. Bernstein, J. B. Rothnie, N. Goodman, C. A. Papadimitriou, "The Concurrency Control Mechanism of SDD-1: A System for Distributed Databases (The Fully Redundant Case)", *IEEE Trans. on Soft. Eng.*, Vol. SE-4, No. 3, May 1978, pp. 154-167.

[BSRG77] P. A. Bernstein, D. W. Shipman, J. B. Rothnie, N. Goodman, "The Concurrency Control Mechanism of SDD-1: A System for Distributed Databases (The General Case)", Comp. Corp. of America Technical Report CCA-77-09, Dec. 1977.

[BSW79] Philip A. Bernstein, David W. Shipman, Wing S. Wong, "Formal Aspects of Serializability in Database Concurrency Control", *IEEE Trans. on Soft. Eng.*, Vol. SE-5, No. 3, May 1979, pp. 203-216.

[BT83a] G. Bracha and S. Toueg, "A Distributed Algorithm for Generalized Deadlock Detection", Dept. of Comp. Sci., Cornell Univ., Tech. Report 83-559, June 1983.

[BT83b] G. Bracha and S. Toueg, "Resilient Consensus Protocols", *Symp. on Prin. of Distributed Sys.*, Montreal, Canada, Aug. 1983, pp. 12-26.

[Brereton83] P. Brereton, "Detection and Resolution of Inconsistencies Among Distributed Replicates of a File", *ACM Operating Systems Review*, Vol. 17, No. 1, Jan. 1983, pp. 10-15.

[Carey83] M. J. Carey, "Granularity Hierarchies in Concurrency Control", *Proc. 2nd ACM Symp. on Prin. of Database Systems*, Atlanta, 21-23 March 1983, pp. 156-165.

[CD73] Edward G. Coffman, Jr., Peter J. Denning, *Operating Systems Theory*, Prentice-Hall, 1973.

[CW75] George R. Couranz, Donald F. Wann, "Theoretical and Experimental Behavior of Synchronizers Operating in the Metastable Region", *IEEE Trans. on Computers*, Vol. C-24, No. 6, June 1975, pp. 604-616.

[Davies73] C. T. Davies, "Recovery Semantics for a DB/DC System", *Proc. ACM Nat'l Conf. 28*, 1973, pp. 136-141.

[Davies78] C. T. Davies, "Data Processing Integrity", from *Computing System Reliability*, Tom Anderson, Brian Randell, eds., Cambridge Univ. Press, 1978, pp. 288-354.

[EGLT76] K. P. Eswaran, J. N. Gray, R. A. Lorie, I. L. Traiger, "The Notion of Consistency and Predicate Locks in a Database System", *Comm. of the ACM*, Vol. 19, No. 11, Nov. 1976, pp. 624-633.

[Garcia-Molina79] Hector Garcia-Molina, "Performance of Update Algorithms for Replicated Data in a Distributed Database", Ph.D. Thesis, Stanford Dept. of Computer Science, available as Stanford Univ. Dept. of Computer Science Report STAN-CS-79-744, June 1979.

[Garcia-Molina82] Hector Garcia-Molina, "Elections in a Distributed Computing System", *IEEE Trans. on Computers*, Vol. C-31, No. 1, Jan. 1982, pp. 48-59.

[Gifford79] David K. Gifford, "Weighted Voting for Replicated Data", *Proc. of 7th Symp. on Operating Systems Principles*, Pacific Grove, CA, Dec. 1979, pp. 150-162.

[Goldman77] B. Goldman, "Deadlock Detection in Computer Networks", S.M. Thesis, M.I.T. Dept. of Elec. Eng. and Comp. Sci., available as M.I.T. Lab. for Comp. Sci. Technical Report 185, Sept. 1977.

[Gray75] J. N. Gray, et al., "Granularity of Locks and Degrees of Consistency in a Shared Data Base", IBM Research Report RJ1654, Sept. 1975.

[Gray78] J. N. Gray, "Notes on Database Operating Systems", in *Lecture Notes in Computer Science*, R. Bayer et al., eds., Springer-Verlag, 1978, pp. 393-481.

[Gray79] J. N. Gray, et al., "The Recovery Manager of a Data Management System", IBM Research Report RJ2623, Aug. 1979.

[Gray80a] J. N. Gray, "Minimizing the Number of Messages in Commit Protocols", IBM Research, San Jose, CA, Sept. 1980 (no report number).

[Gray80b] J. N. Gray, photocopies of transparencies for a talk concerning experience with System R, 1980.

[Gray81] J. N. Gray, et al., "The Recovery Manager of the System R Database Manager", *ACM Computing Surveys*, Vol. 13, No. 2, June 1981, pp. 223-242.

[GS80] Virgil D. Gligor, Susan H. Shattuck, "On Deadlock Detection in Distributed Systems", *IEEE Trans. on Soft. Eng.*, Vol. SE-6, No. 5, Sept. 1980, pp. 435-440.

[HS80] Michael Hammer and David Shipman, "Reliability Mechanisms for SDD-1: A System for Distributed Databases", *ACM Trans. on Database Sys.*, Vol. 5, No. 4, Dec. 1980, pp. 431-466.

[IM80] Sreekaanth S. Isloor, T. Anthony Marsland, "The Deadlock Problem: An Overview", *IEEE Computer Magazine*, Vol. 13, No. 9, Sept. 1980, pp. 58-78.

[IMS78] J. Israel, J. Mitchell, H. Sturgis, "Separating Data from Function in a Distributed File System", *Proc. 2nd Int'l Symp. on Operating Systems*, IRIA, 1978; to appear in D. Lanciaux, ed., *Operating Systems*, North Holland.

[Jessop82] W. H. Jessop, et al., "The EDEN Transaction-Based File System", *Proc 2nd IEEE Symp. on Reliability in Distributed Software and Database Systems*, Pittsburgh, July 19-21 1982, pp. 163-170.

[Korth81] Henry F. Korth, "A Deadlock Free, Variable Granularity Locking Protocol", *Proc. of the 5th Berkeley Workshop on Distributed Data Management and Computer Networks*, Berkeley, CA, Feb. 1981.

[Korth82a] H. F. Korth, "Edge Locks and Deadlock Avoidance in Distributed Systems", *ACM SIGACT-SIGOPS Symp. on Prin. of Distributed Computing*, Ottawa, Canada, 18-20 Aug 1983, pp. 173-182.

[Korth82b] H. F. Korth, "Deadlock Freedom Using Edge Locks", *ACM Trans. on Database Systems*, Vol. 7, No. 4, Dec. 1982, pp. 632-652.

[KR81] H. T. Kung and J. T. Robinson, "On Optimistic Methods for Concurrency Control", *ACM Trans. on Database Sys.*, Vol. 6, No. 2, June 1981, pp. 213-226.

[Lamport78] Leslie Lamport, "Time, Clocks, and the Ordering of Events in a Distributed System", *Comm. of the ACM*, Vol. 21, No. 7, July 1978, pp. 558-565.

[Lazowska81] E. D. Lazowska, et al., "The Architecture of the EDEN System", *Proc. 8th ACM Symp. on Operating System Prin.*, Dec. 1981, pp. 148-159.

[LeLann81] LeLann, Gerard, "A Distributed System for Real-Time Transaction Processing", *IEEE Computer Magazine*, Vol. 14, No. 2, Feb. 1981, pp. 43-48.

[LFF82] N. Lynch, M. Fischer, and R. Fowler, "A Simple and Efficient Byzantine Generals Algorithm", *Proc. 2nd Symp. on Reliability in Distributed Software and Database Sys.*, Pittsburgh, Pa., July 1982, pp. 46-52.

[LGH80] P. A. Lee, N. Ghani, K. Heron, "A Recovery Cache for the PDP-11", *IEEE Trans. on Computers*, Vol. C-29, No. 6, June 1980, pp. 546-549.

[Lindsay79] Bruce Lindsay, et al., "Notes on Distributed Databases", IBM Research Report RJ2571, July 1979.

[Lindsay84] Bruce Lindsay, et al., "Computation and Communication in R*: A Distributed Data Manager", *ACM Trans. on Comp. Systems*, Vol. 2, No. 1, Feb. 1984, pp. 24-38.

[Liskov79] Barbara H. Liskov, "Primitives for Distributed Computing", *Proc. 7th Symp. on Operating System Principles*, Pacific Grove, CA, Dec. 1979, pp. 33-42.

[Liskov81] B. Liskov, et al. *CLU Reference Manual*, Springer-Verlag, New York, 1981.

[Liskov82] Barbara H. Liskov, "On Linguistic Support for Distributed Programming", *IEEE Trans. on Software Engineering*, Vol. SE-8, No. 3, May 1982, pp. 203-210.

[LL83] R. C. Lian and M. T. Liu, "Cells: An Approach to Design of a Fault Tolerant Network Operating System", *Proc. 3rd IEEE Symp. on Reliability in Distributed Software and Database Systems*, Clearwater Beach, Fa., Oct. 17-19 1983, pp. 75-79.

[LM83] B. Liskov and M. Herlihy, "Issues in Process and Communication Structure for Distributed Programs", *Proc. 3rd IEEE Symp. on Reliability in Distributed Software and Database Systems*, Clearwater Beach, Fa., Oct. 17-19 1983, pp. 123-132.

[Lomet77] D. B. Lomet, "Process Structuring, Synchronization, and Recovery Using Atomic Actions", *Proc. ACM Conf. on Language Design for Reliable Software*, ACM Sigplan Notices, Vol. 12, No. 3, March 1977, pp. 128-137.

[LS] Butler Lampson and Howard Sturgis, "Crash Recovery in a Distributed Data Storage System", to appear in *Comm. of the ACM*.

[LS83] B. Liskov and R. Scheifler, "Guardians and Actions: Linguistic Support for Robust Distributed Programs", *ACM Trans. on Prog. Lang. and Systems*, Vol. 5, No. 3, July 1983, pp. 381-404.

[LS84] Y.-H. Lee and K. G. Shin, "Design and Evaluation of A Fault-Tolerant Multiprocessor Using Hardware Recovery Blocks", *IEEE Trans. on Comp.*, Vol. C-33, No. 2, Feb. 1984, pp. 113-124.

[LSP82] L. Lamport, R. Shostak, and M. Pease, "The Byzantine Generals Problem", *ACM Trans. on Prog. Lang. and Sys.*, Vol. 4, No. 3, July 1982, pp. 382-401.

[Lynch83] N. A. Lynch, "Concurrency Control for Resilient Nested Transactions", *Proc. 2nd ACM SIGACT-SOGMOD Symp. on Prin. of Database Sys.*, Atlanta, Mar. 1983, pp. 166-181.

[MAT83] M. S. McKendry, J. E. Allchin, and W. C. Thibault, "Architecture for a Global Operating System", *Proc. IEEE Infocom '83*, May 1983, pp. 25-30.

[MM79] Daniel A. Menasce, Richard R. Muntz, "Locking and Deadlock Detection in Distributed Data Bases", *IEEE Trans. on Soft. Eng.*, Vol. SE-5, No. 3, May 1979, pp. 195-202.

[MMP83] E. T. Mueller, J. D. Moore, and G. J. Popek, "A Nested Transaction Mechanism for LOCUS", *Proc. 9th ACM Symp. on Operating Systems Principles*, Bretton Woods, NH, Oct. 10-13 1983, pp. 71-89.

[Montgomery78] W. A. Montgomery, "Robust Concurrency Control for a Distributed Information System", Ph.D. Thesis, M.I.T. Dept. of Elec. Eng. and Comp. Sci., available as M.I.T. Lab. for Comp. Sci. Technical Report 207, Dec. 1978.

[Moss81] J. Eliot B. Moss, "Nested Transactions: An Approach to Reliable Distributed Computing", Ph.D. Thesis, M.I.T. Dept. of Elec. Eng. and Comp. Sci., available as M.I.T. Lab. for Comp. Sci. Technical Report 260, April 1981.

[Moss83] E. Moss, "Checkpoint and Restart in Distributed Transaction Systems", *Proc. 3rd IEEE Symp. on Reliability in Distributed Software and Database Systems*, Clearwater Beach, Fla., Oct. 19-21 1983, pp. 85-89.

[Needham83] R. M. Needham, et al., "How to Connect Stable Memory to a Computer", *ACM Operating Systems Review*, Vol. 17, No. 1, Jan. 1983, p. 16.

[Obermarck80] Ron Obermarck, "Global Deadlock Detection Algorithm", IBM report RJ2845, June 1980.

[PK82] C. H. Papadimitriou and P. C. Kanellakis, "On Concurrency Control by Multiple Versions", *Proc. ACM Symp. on Prin. of Database Systems*, Los Angeles, 29-31 March, 1982, pp. 76-82; also available as *ACM Trans. on Database Systems*, Vol. 9, No. 1, March, 1984, pp. 89-99.

[Paxton79] William H. Paxton, "A Client-Based Transaction System to Maintain Data Integrity", *Proc. of 7th Symp. on Operating System Principles*, Pacific Grove, CA, Dec. 1979, pp. 18-23.

[Popek81] G. Popek, et al., "LOCUS: A Network Transparent, High Reliability Distributed System", *Proc. 8th Symp. on Operating Systems Principles*, Dec. 1981, pp. 169-177.

[Reed78] David P. Reed, "Naming and Synchronization in a Decentralized Computer System", Ph.D. Thesis, M.I.T. Dept. of Elec. Eng. and Comp. Sci., available as M.I.T. Lab. for Comp. Sci. Technical Report 205, Sept. 1978.

[RLT78] B. Randell, P. A. Lee, P. C. Treleaven, "Reliability Issues in Computing System Design", *ACM Computing Surveys*, Vol. 10, No. 2, June 1978, pp. 123-165.

[RSL78] Daniel J. Rosenkrantz, Richard E. Stearns, Philip M. Lewis II, "System Level Concurrency Control for Distributed Systems", *ACM Trans. on Database Systems*, Vol. 3, No. 2, June 1978, pp. 178-198.

[Russell80] David L. Russell, "State Restoration in Systems of Communicating Processes", *IEEE Trans. on Soft. Eng.*, Vol. SE-6, No. 2, March 1980, pp. 183-194.

[Schneider84] F. B. Schneider, "Byzantine Generals in Action: Implementing Fail-Stop Processors", *ACM Trans. on Comp. Sys.*, Vol. 2, No. 2, May 1984, pp. 145-154.

[Silberschatz82] A. Silberschatz, "A Multi-Version Concurrency Control Scheme With No Rollbacks", *ACM SIGACT-SIGOPS Symp. on Prin. of Distributed Computing*, Ottawa, Canada, Aug. 18-20, 1982, pp. 216-223.

[SMB79] Daniel Swinehart, Gene McDaniel, David Boggs, "WFS: A Simple Shared File System for a Distributed Environment", *Proc. of 7th Symp. on Operating System Principles*, Pacific Grove, CA, Dec. 1979, pp. 9-17.

[SRC81] J. H. Saltzer, D. P. Reed, D. D. Clark, "End-to-end Arguments in System Design", *Proceedings of the 2nd Int'l Conf. on Distributed Computing Systems*, Versailles, France, April 1981.

[Stonebraker79] Michael Stonebraker, "Concurrency Control and Consistency of Multiple Copies of Data in Distributed INGRES", *IEEE Trans. on Soft. Eng.*, Vol. SE-5, No. 3, May 1979, pp. 188-194.

[SY84] Rob Strom and Shaula Yemini, private communication and unpublished papers, IBM Research, Yorktown Heights, NY, 1984.

[Svobodova80] Liba Svobodova, "Management of Object Histories in the Swallow Repository", M.I.T. Lab. for Comp. Sci. Technical Report 243, July 1980.

[Takagi79] Akihiro Takagi, "Concurrent and Reliable Updates of Distributed Databases", M.I.T. Lab. for Comp. Sci. Technical Memo 144, Nov. 1979, submitted to *Comm. of the ACM*.

[Thomas79] R. H. Thomas, "A Majority Consensus Approach to Concurrency Control for Multiple Copy Databases", *ACM Trans. on Database Systems*, Vol. 4, No. 2, June 1979, pp. 180-209.

[Verhofstad78] J. S. M. Verhofstad, "Recovery Techniques for Database Systems", *ACM Computing Surveys*, Vol. 10, No. 2, June 1978, pp. 167-195.

[Williams81] R. Williams, et al., "R*: An Overview of the Architecture", *Improving Usability and Responsiveness*, P. Scheurman, ed., Academic Press, New York, pp. 1-27, also available as IBM Research Report RJ3325, San Jose, Dec. 1981.

[WP83] B. Walker, G. Popek, et al., "The LOCUS Distributed Operating System", *Proc. 9th ACM Symp. on Operating System Principles*, Bretton Woods, NH, Oct. 10-13 1983, pp. 49-70.

[Wright83] D. D. Wright, "Managing Distributed Databases in Partitioned Networks", Ph.D. thesis, Dept. of Comp. Sci., Cornell Univ., TR 83-572, Sept. 1983.

[WS83] D. D. Wright and D. Skeen, "Merging Partitioned Databases", Dept. of Comp. Sci., Cornell Univ., TR 83-547, Aug. 1983.

[Zobel83] D. Zobel, "The Deadlock Problem: A Classifying Bibliography", *ACM Operating Systems Review*, Vol. 17, No. 4, Oct. 1983, pp. 6-15.

Author and Citation Index

Subject Index

The MIT Press, with Peter Denning as consulting editor, publishes computer science books in the following series:

ACM Doctoral Dissertation Award and Distinguished Dissertation Series
Artificial Intelligence, Patrick Winston and Michael Brady, editors
Charles Babbage Institute Reprint Series for the History of Computing, Martin Campbell-Kelly, editor
Computer Systems, Herb Schwetman, editor
Foundations of Computing, Michael Garey, editor
History of Computing, I. Bernard Cohen, editor, and William Aspray, associate editor
Information Systems, Michael Lesk, editor
Scientific Computation, Dennis Gannon. editor
The MIT Electrical Engineering and Computer Science Series

For information on submission of manuscripts for publication, call or write to:
Frank P. Satlow
Executive Editor, Computer Science and Engineering
The MIT Press
28 Carleton Street
Cambridge, MA 02142
617-253-1623